FRIENDLY POLITICS

How We the People Can Stop Hating Each Other, Have Productive Conversations, and Actually Get Things Done

Glen Smith

MUSINE

ISBN: **978-1-63161-191-9**

Sign up for Glen Smith's newsletter at
www.disagreeingagreeably.com/newsletter

MUSINE

Published by Musine
An Imprint of TCK Publishing
www.TCKpublishing.com

Get discounts and special deals on our best selling books at
www.TCKpublishing.com/bookdeals

Check out additional discounts for bulk orders at
www.TCKpublishing.com/bulk-book-orders

DISCLAIMER

Discussing politics might make you feel angry, upset, or overwhelmed. But reading this book may actually make politics fun again. Proceed with caution. ;)

TABLE OF CONTENTS

CHAPTER 1

Introduction

"There is nothing which I dread so much as the division
of the republic into two great parties."

—John Adams

Does thinking about politics make you worried, frustrated,
or angry? Have you stopped associating with friends or
relatives because of political disagreements? Do you avoid
talking about politics because you fear it will make others
mad? Are you frustrated because politicians are incapable
of getting things done? Is there any part of you that fears
the end of America is right around the corner?

If you answered yes to any of these questions, you
are the victim of a mental illness. Although you may not
have the illness yourself, it nonetheless harms your life and
threatens to destroy your country.

For those who suffer from it, this illness creates
devastating consequences in their personal lives, and
impacts the wellbeing of their loved ones. It makes
people believe in an alternate reality that stops them from
acting in their own best interests. Victims of the disorder
suffer from the loss of valuable friendships and become
estranged from family members. In extreme cases, some
of the inflicted commit violent acts, dehumanize others,

and support government suppression of fundamental rights and liberties. This mental disorder is especially insidious because it works subtly, in unseen ways, so that those living under its influence are not even aware they have a problem. You, like hundreds of millions of other Americans, may well be under its effects right now and not even realize it.

Unlike other mental disorders, this one is especially likely to affect those who hold political power. By interfering with the judgment and competence of key decision-makers, this mental illness makes it more difficult for governments to address large-scale social, economic, and environmental problems. If you've ever felt like our government wasn't doing a good job, this disorder is one of the reasons why. If left untreated, the ultimate prognosis for this mental disorder is the end of American democracy in favor of an oppressive dictatorship.

Unfortunately, this disorder is not some hypothetical scenario, or a storyline from a bad science fiction novel. The mental disorder I just described is an irrational form of political *partisanship*. It is not an exaggeration to say that this disorder has already done widespread damage to millions of lives, caused thousands of unnecessary deaths, and continues to rapidly destroy the foundation of American democracy.

So what do I mean by "partisanship?" What I'm talking about here is an emotional allegiance to a political party that is often "blind, prejudiced, and unreasoning"[1]. Those afflicted see the world as divided into blue and red—Democrat and Republican. They have an irrational fear of the opposing party gaining political power, and they often ruminate on catastrophic thoughts like, "If that person wins the election, the world will end."

Partisanship results in a dogmatic adherence to the opinions, thoughts, and beliefs of one side regardless of the reality of the present circumstances and situations involved. In many cases, it becomes increasingly irrational and destructive over time and grows into a bona fide mental disorder, which eventually causes unforeseen negative effects on individual lives, relationships, and society. Although not currently an established mental disorder, I will explain in the next chapter how partisanship fits the accepted definition of one, and how its consequences are just as destructive as those of clinically accepted mental illnesses.

It is important to note that, as with all dysfunctions, partisanship is not *inherently* unhealthy and destructive. Preferring one party over another—or consistently voting for one party—is not necessarily a bad thing. Political parties serve important functions in government, and candidate party affiliations allow voters to make more informed decisions. Just as a person who indulges over the holidays doesn't suddenly become obese, partisanship exists on a spectrum, with rationality on one end and irrationality on the other. In Chapter 3, I'll dive into more detail about what distinguishes rational party affiliation from irrational partisanship.

Simply put, the purpose of this book is to cure irrational partisanship in individuals and society at large. Admittedly, that's a large task, but it is possible for each of us to reflect on our true values and change the way we think, interact, and make decisions for the good of ourselves and each other. This book provides a variety of scientifically proven techniques—with insights from numerous disciplines such as political science, philosophy, psychiatry, psychology, and communication science—that will help prevent partisanship from harming your life. Some of the techniques we'll discuss have also proven effective in treating other mental disorders, such as anxiety, depression, and substance abuse, while others are derived from scientifically validated research on cognitive bias, media influence, and interpersonal communication.

Even if you do not consider yourself a partisan (few people do), this book will help you to effectively deal with partisans you encounter. Too many Americans have unnecessarily lost friends and avoided contact with relatives because of political disagreements.[2] Although grumpy misanthropes such as myself often desire to become better strangers with the rest of humanity, most people value interpersonal relationships as one of the most important things in their lives. If politics has hurt your relationships with friends, family, or romantic partners, this book can help you soften those hard feelings and protect your relationships in the future. After all, if you can't deal with disagreement, your most valued relationships are always just one argument or social media post from coming to an end in bitter hostility and indefinite silence.

Reading this book will also help you talk about politics in a friendly, civil, and constructive manner. Unfortunately, many people avoid political discussion like the plague.[3] This is a shame, considering that open political discussion has the power to make you more thoughtful, empathetic, connected to your community, and an all-around better citizen.[4]

If talking about politics usually makes your eyes burn with rage, this book can give you a new perspective on political disagreement that will cool your internal fire. No matter what your situation, the tactics and perspectives you'll find can help you participate in productive political discussions without getting angry or frustrated. Never again will you dread political conversations at work, parties, barbecues, or Thanksgiving dinner. In fact, you might even look forward to them once you learn the new strategies that we'll explore together.

Perhaps most importantly, this book will provide you with ways to help change the American political system to save democracy. We need to confront partisanship on an individual level in our own lives, but it is also critical that we fix the underlying issues in our political institutions that created this destructive disorder in the first place.

The primary cause of irrational partisanship is an electoral system that forces voters to choose between the lesser of two evils from the two dominant parties.[5] Changing the electoral system is an essential step in reducing fear of the opposing party and stopping the most destructive aspects of partisanship.

Obviously, partisanship is not the only reason people hate each other. Political disagreements stir up hostility for a variety of other reasons. Social divisions over wealth, culture, race, religion, and geography can generate fear, anger, and hatred. It is not the purpose of this book to address every single source of political animosity. Although partisanship is just one cause of political hostility, it currently overlaps with most other divisions within the United States, and it prevents us from addressing problems rooted in other social divisions. We will not solve the global warming crisis until we can talk about it in a constructive way. The same is true for gun violence, poverty, international conflicts, or any other problem where the two parties disagree (which is every problem!). The widespread and deep-seated mistrust of those who disagree with our views makes it very difficult to come to any legitimately beneficial solutions to our nation's problems.

Curing partisanship is a necessary step toward addressing the seemingly intractable problems we face as a human race. This book will help point to the root sources of partisanship and illuminate the more effective ways to address and treat the problem.

Why I Wrote This Book

Regret is a unique aspect of the human condition. When I look back on my life, I have many regrets over mistakes I've made and opportunities I've missed. But so many of my life experiences—even some of the most difficult and painful ones—were necessary to get me where I am today. And those same life experiences led me to write this book. Over the course of my life so far, I have experienced what it's like to be a hardcore Republican, a radical Democrat, and (currently) a pragmatic nonpartisan.

At one point, I hated Democrats and thought they were stupid, pretentious, and unrealistic; at another point, I hated Republicans and believed they were evil, heartless racists. Now, I don't feel anger or hatred toward members of either party. Instead, I feel empathy for those suffering from the same partisanship that afflicted me earlier in life. If I were to hate some Democrats or Republicans for being irrational, hateful, or ignorant, I would have to hate myself as well. I don't hate that previous version of myself;

instead, I feel pity for his ignorance and the illness that corrupted his thinking. My hope is that by reading this book, you'll gain a healthier view of, and relationship with, yourself and with people who support the opposing party.

As if my political life weren't crazy enough, my personal life gave me an intimate understanding of particular mental disorders. My childhood was filled with domestic violence and unrelenting economic uncertainty. I knew I could be homeless at any moment, and thus found myself living with an anxiety disorder most of my life. In my early thirties, I suffered periods of severe depression. But do you know what changed my life? I stumbled across a book that completely altered my perspective of my problems: *How to Control Your Anxiety Before It Controls You* by Albert Ellis (more on Ellis in Chapter 8). This book appealed to me because it did not offer mysticism or pseudo-science to solve my problems. Instead, Ellis simply offered rationality and a different way of looking at the world. The book showed me that my problems were a direct result of my ignorance, irrational beliefs, and unrealistic expectations. Like many others, I suffered from destructive "-ations," such as exaggerations, overgeneralizations, and simplifications. As you will see, rationality can cure partisanship, just as it can help cure anxiety and depression.

The experiences from my political and personal journeys helped me notice the similarities between the grip of partisanship and other mental illnesses. It is only because I experienced both that I came to understand how partisanship exerts power to manipulate and influence the human mind. My struggles with partisanship and anxiety are what motivated me to find legitimate, useful strategies that can effectively help you avoid the damage of partisanship in your life and the lives of those you care about.

My goal is to show you how much improvement can come from a simple change in perspective. Words have the power to reveal things; to shine a slightly different light on the world in a way that changes everything. Once you have seen the world from that new perspective, your eyes will open, and you will never look at things the same way again. You leave the cave and see the sun for the first time. You take the red pill and travel down the rabbit hole. Reading this book will give you a new, healthier, and more illuminated perspective that will not just change how you feel about politics, but how you feel about yourself, others, and the amazing world we all share together.

I have spent most of my life studying political psychology, partisan media, and political hostility. By chance alone, I happened to attend one of the few Doctoral Programs in the world that specializes in political psychology. After falling in love with the topic, I went on to research the causes of political hatred. Throughout my career as a professor of American politics, I have taught thousands of students how to discuss politics in productive ways. I have been interviewed by prominent television, radio, and newspaper outlets, have authored numerous academic journal articles, and wrote a textbook called *Disagreeing Agreeably: Issue Debates with a Primer on Political Hostility*. While *Disagreeing Agreeably* is an academic text aimed at college students, I wanted to write a book that could help anyone deal with political disagreement more effectively. It is with that purpose in mind that this book was born. I strongly believe that if you give this book a chance, it will help you create meaningful, positive changes in your life.

How This Book Can Help You

This book is composed of three parts. The first part looks at the destructive character of partisanship and its current role in American politics. We'll also explore the incredible evidence showing that partisanship meets the criteria for a bona fide mental illness. Chapter 3 makes the important distinction between "rational" and "irrational" partisanship. In brief, partisanship becomes an illness when your desire to see your party win corrupts how you think and causes pervasive harm to your life and to society. While rational partisanship can help you make better political decisions, irrational partisanship warps the way you see the world, increases hatred and discrimination, and makes you less likely to achieve your goals.

In the second part of this book, we'll explore where partisanship comes from. Understanding the roots of this illness will highlight solutions that actually stand a chance of working. Each chapter in Part Two addresses a specific cause of irrational partisanship and concludes with simple techniques to fix the problem. Chapter 4 explains the key social factors that lead to irrational partisanship and how they create the illusion that Americans are genuinely divided up into us vs. them, good vs. evil, Democrats vs. Republicans. The fictitious narrative that Americans are either red or blue is simply an illusion that has been trumpeted by politicians and the news media. As Chapter 5 shows, this belief makes partisans too reliant on politicians and media personalities, who paint members of the opposing party as stupid, immoral, untrustworthy, and generally inferior human beings. Because of this, partisanship eventually breeds prejudicial disgust and mistrust of people we see as allied to the other party, which can result in dehumanization, political violence, and a willingness to suppress the rights and freedoms of the opposition. In Chapter 6, I'll explain how the belief that members of the other party are evil creates an unconscious motivation to believe *anything* that keeps them from gaining political power. This pattern leads to poor decision making, inconsistency, emotional volatility, delusions, and self-defeating behaviors. But because this mental illness works subtly, partisans fail to realize when partisanship is causing harm in their lives. Similar to other mental disorders, our minds protect us from recognizing the problem, even as it tears our lives apart.

Part Three of this book examines promising ways to effectively address partisanship in American society. First, Chapter 7 explains how intellectual humility can inoculate people against the irrational form of partisanship. You can achieve intellectual humility by recognizing the limitations of your understanding, acknowledging your potential biases, and (most importantly) accepting that you might be wrong. Chapter 8 discusses how a common therapeutic approach called Rational Emotive Behavior Therapy (REBT) can treat irrational partisanship. While REBT is an effective treatment for anxiety, depression, and substance abuse, I'll explain how it can easily be applied to treating partisanship as well.

As with other mental illnesses, social institutions also play a role in instigating the illness. In Chapter 9, I'll discuss how partisan media feed irrational partisanship. Fortunately, simple modifications in your news consumption can not only reduce your fear of the other party, but also help you become better informed about political affairs. Chapter 10 then discusses potential reforms that can be implemented in political institutions in order to reduce irrational partisanship in the American public. Although these reforms are not meant to change the partisan balance of power, they do change the rules of the political game, which can break the psychological hold of partisanship on the political system.

Finally, Chapter 11 will equip you to discuss politics in a civil, friendly, mutually enriching, and productive manner. Rather than avoiding political discussions with friends, relatives, and coworkers, you can look forward to learning what others think, hearing about different perspectives, and coming away from conversations with a sense of growth and contentment instead of hostility and resentment.

Treatment: Assess the Problem

At the end of each chapter, I will provide a task, or "treatment," that will help this book have a more positive effect on your life. To get the most from these treatments, I recommend writing down your responses. Most of the tasks in each future chapter build upon treatments in previous chapters, so it will be helpful to record your responses. I promise that you'll see significant progress and changes by the end of this book. You'll be happy you kept a record, whether you use pen and paper or an electronic device.

Now it's time for your first treatment: the Partisanship Quiz! Just write down your answers to the questions below. It is very important that you be honest with yourself; after all, no one will see your answers. Think of this as one of those online questionnaires that assesses your personality traits, evaluates your alcohol dependence, or tells you whether you're a sociopath (yes, I've taken all of those quizzes and I'm happy to say I scored low in sociopathy). This quiz is not meant to make you feel judged, but rather assesses how susceptible you are to irrational partisanship. It'll be a lot easier to get where you want to go when you have a clearer picture of where you're starting from. You can also use this quiz to determine whether people you know suffer from irrational partisanship, and would benefit from the book as a birthday present.

Partisanship Quiz

Using the scale below, write down a number from 0 to 100 that reflects how you feel about the people described. Scores closer to 0 mean you generally feel negative and cold toward those people, while scores closer to 100 mean you feel positive and warm toward them.

0 – 10 – 20 – 30 – 40 – 50 – 60 – 70 – 80 – 90 – 100

NEGATIVE/COLD   POSITIVE/WARM

- Write down a number that reflects how you feel about Democrats in Congress.

- Write down a number that reflects how you feel about Republicans in Congress.

- (If the absolute difference between the two numbers above exceeds 50, you might be a partisan.)

- Write down a number that reflects how you feel about people who usually vote for Democrats.

- Write down a number that reflects how you feel about people who usually vote for Republicans.

- (Again, if the absolute difference exceeds 50, you might have a problem.)

Answer whether you believe each of the following statements are true or false. If you affiliate with neither party, replace "other Party" in each question with the Party you dislike the most.

- True or False: The other Party wants to destroy what is great about America.

- True or False: Most people in the other Party are close-minded.

- True or False: Most people in the other Party are ignorant.

- True or False: Most people in the other Party are intolerant.

- True or False: I can't understand why anyone would vote for the other party.

- True or False: America would be better off if the other party left the country.

- True or False: I often feel hatred toward people who vote for the other party.

The more times you answered "True" to the questions above, the more likely you suffer from an unhealthy form of partisanship. A high score doesn't necessarily mean you suffer from a mental illness, but higher scores do indicate you are at higher risk of suffering negative consequences in your life, and possibly affecting others in a negative way. Any score higher than 3 suggests you might have a problem.

CHAPTER 2

Why Partisanship Is a Mental Disorder

"In individuals, insanity is rare; but in groups, parties, nations, and epochs, it is the rule."

—Friedrich Nietzsche

Is partisanship really a mental disorder? Does it actually matter whether we categorize it as such? It does matter to an extent, because the answers to these questions influence how society and our governments respond to the problem. This chapter examines the claim that partisanship is a mental disorder, as well as its implications. If you already believe that extreme partisanship is a mental illness and need no convincing, I still hope you'll take the time to read this chapter because you may not understand the true scope of the problems partisanship causes for individuals and society.

What makes something a mental disorder? When I first looked into this question, I was surprised by the lack of clarity involved in categorizing mental disorders. To be blunt, the criteria seem quite vague, ambiguous, and widely applicable to a variety of mental processes.

Officially, according to the American Psychiatric Association:

A mental disorder is a syndrome characterized by clinically significant disturbance in an individual's cognition, emotion regulation, or behavior that reflects a dysfunction in the psychological, biological, or developmental processes underlying mental functioning. Mental disorders are usually associated with significant distress in social, occupational, or other important activities. An expectable or culturally approved response to a common stressor or loss, such as the death of a loved one, is not a mental disorder. Socially deviant behavior (e.g., political, religious, or sexual) and conflicts that are primarily between the individual and society are not mental disorders unless the deviance or conflict results from a dysfunction in the individual, as described above.[6]

This definition points to two fundamental criteria that determine whether an individual is suffering from a mental disorder. First, mental disorders (or illnesses) are a "clinically significant disturbance in an individual's cognition, emotion regulation, or behavior that reflects a dysfunction in the psychological, biological, or developmental processes underlying mental functioning." The problematic word here is "dysfunction." In order to identify something as "dysfunctional," you first need a functional state to compare it to. In other words, to call something a mental disorder, we must first compare it to a healthy state of mental well-being. In Chapter 3, I will explain what a functional (rational) form of partisanship looks like and compare it to the dysfunctional (irrational) form of partisanship that afflicts millions of Americans.

As for the second criterion, a mental disorder must result in outcomes that are damaging and counterproductive to your basic goals in life. Specifically, the outcomes are "usually associated with significant distress in social, occupational, or other important activities." Past research shows that strong identification with a political party puts a strain on personal relationships, causes estrangement from family members, negatively affects romantic relationships, and even biases employers' hiring decisions.[7] This is the element that most of this chapter focuses on: the unhealthy and undesirable outcomes partisanship has on individuals and on society. As I explain in this chapter and throughout the rest of the book, there is sufficient evidence that dysfunctional partisanship meets both of these requirements for mental illness.

Make no mistake, the data are clear and unambiguous: partisanship has dangerous consequences at the individual level, the societal level, and at the level of government effectiveness. Evidence increasingly shows that partisanship heavily influences how we live our lives.[8]

Too many of us just flat-out don't like members of the other party and are genuinely afraid of what will happen if the other party gains political power. In a 2019 survey from the Pew Research Center, partisans were asked to record their feelings toward people in the opposite party.[9] A dramatic majority (79 percent of Democrats, 83 percent of Republicans) gave the other side a negative score, judging them as "very cold" on the scale. It's important to note that things weren't always this way—but since the 1980s, partisans on both sides have adopted increasingly negative views of the opposing party.[10] As a result, partisans are more afraid than ever about what (they believe) would happen if the other party gained power. Just before the 2020 election, roughly *90 percent* of both Biden and Trump supporters believed that if the other candidate won the election, it would "lead to lasting harm to the United States."[11]

Furthermore, America is unique in the way its partisan divide reaches so many non-political issues and concerns. While partisanship exists in other countries, only in the US does it seem to influence nearly every aspect of our lives, both political and non-political.[12] For example, these negative feelings between the parties significantly impact our ability to connect and interact with others. Partisans often see members of the opposing party as fundamentally different people; they believe members of the other party don't even share their non-political values and goals.[13] In fact, most partisans believe that members of the opposing party are not even *approachable*, which pretty much precludes getting to truly know and understand them.[14]

This mutual distaste helps explain why partisans are less likely to seek out friendships with members of the opposing party.[15] During the 2020 election, *less than a quarter* of supporters for either presidential candidate claimed to have more than a few friends who supported the other candidate.[16] How well can you really understand other perspectives if you don't even know members of the other party?

Partisanship also causes family estrangement.[17] One study even found that political disagreement made people spend substantially less time at Thanksgiving with their relatives—collectively 34 million fewer hours in 2016 alone.[18] Now don't get me wrong, I'm all in favor of avoiding extended family during the holidays if that's the route we want to go. But if we can't even tolerate talking politics for a few hours with certain family members once a year, what hope is there for us to ever have open discussions with neighbors, coworkers, or local leaders? How will we ever find a solution or understand each other if we can't even talk to one another? In short, partisanship is straining valuable and important personal relationships, limiting social interactions, ending friendships, and estranging family members.

Partisanship also has potentially devastating consequences on our romantic lives. Studies show that partisans actively seek out romantic partners who share their political preferences, effectively cutting their pool of potential partners in half.[19] Partisanship has become so dominant a force on our emotions that it even affects who we're attracted to! In one experiment, researchers asked participants to rate the attractiveness of people in photos, but they altered the party identification of the person in the picture. Partisans were less likely to say members of the opposing party were attractive—even when looks were held constant.[20] As if that weren't enough of an obstacle, parents are also less likely to approve of their child marrying someone from the opposite party. Again, this wasn't always so. Back in 1960, only 5 percent of Republicans and 4 percent of Democrats said they would be displeased if their son or daughter married someone affiliated with an opposing party; by 2010, those numbers jumped to 49 percent and 33 percent, respectively.[21] It's hard enough to find a happy, romantic relationship without automatically disqualifying half the country!

If I had chosen to date my wife based on political agreement, we never would have married. She and I are very different people—so different in fact, it's hard to imagine how we've maintained a successful and loving marriage since our early twenties. My wife was raised in a very religious family; I was not. She's a music teacher who can play almost every instrument, while my five-year-old son knows more about music than I do. I am introverted, cranky, disorganized, and neurotic; she is an extroverted, pleasant, over-organized delight. Why are we together? Simply put, we have the same sense of humor, so we make each other laugh. In fact, that is the one consistent feature of every successful romantic relationship I have ever seen. Yet to find out if someone shares your sense of humor, you have to actually spend time getting to know them. You have to give them a chance. Avoiding people because of political differences completely shuts off any possibility of getting to know them in the ways that really matter.

Beyond relationships, partisanship also weakens our ability to make personal decisions. One reason for this is that Democrats and Republicans each live in very different worlds. This belief alters the lens through which they filter reality, which biases their decisions in sometimes dangerous ways. In fact, partisanship can even lead us to hold fundamentally different *factual beliefs*. Large portions of both Democrats and Republicans believe "facts" that are simply not true, and disbelieve or minimize facts that are actually correct. When we prioritize party lines, we tend to believe any evidence so long as it either supports our party or harms the other party, with little regard for reality.[22]

To give you an example of how partisanship can change the way two people see the same facts, let's look at the national economy. Studies show that partisanship can alter our beliefs about how the economy performed in the past year.[23] All things equal, partisans tend to believe the economy is doing better when their party is in power, regardless of actual economic indicators.[24] As the authors of one study explain, "Republicans and Democrats, because of their partisan lenses, are not fully objective observers and evaluators of the economy—too ready to see the good signs when their party controls the White House, and too ready to ignore the good signs when the other party is in charge."[25] These biased economic evaluations can have important consequences for personal finances as well as voting behaviors. Think about it: your perceptions of the economy probably influence a number of important financial decisions, such as whether and how you invest in the stock market, take a vacation, buy a home, change jobs, start a business, or expand a current one. Allowing irrational partisanship to distort your perceptions of the economy can have long-term consequences for your life and the national economy.

Partisanship also leads to discrimination in professional and consumer behavior. Whether acting as consumers, employers, or fellow citizens, partisans discriminate against opposing partisans. They're more likely to buy things from members of their own party, and to avoid dealing with members of the opposing party. One study found that if you're a partisan, you're more likely to demand a raise if you learn your boss supports the opposing party, and also "less likely to purchase a heavily discounted gift card if the seller was affiliated with the other party."[26] To this point, partisanship also leads to economic discrimination among employers. One study mailed out job applications in response to various Help Wanted ads, changing the party identification of the applicant by indicating that they were a member of either College Democrats or College Republicans.[27] Their findings? Employers were less likely to contact applicants from the opposing political party. Partisans are also willing to discriminate against members of the opposing party when reviewing applications for college admissions and scholarships.[28] How would you feel about being denied valuable opportunities simply because the person evaluating you belonged to a different political party? Can you think of any time you may have let someone's politics affect your judgement of their abilities?

Perhaps most alarmingly, evidence indicates that partisanship increases support for lawlessness, as long as the victims belong to (or at least seem to belong to) the opposing group. Partisans are always concerned when the other party engages in (illegal) electoral tricks—such as stealing yard signs or calling people with deceptive election information—but they're less concerned when members of their own party engage in the *exact same* illegal behavior.[29]

What's more, research suggests that partisans are even willing to support, or at least justify, *violence* against opposing partisans.[30] This is certainly consistent with partisan responses to recent violent protests sparked by either Democratic- or Republican-leaning groups. Regardless of whether or not they actively participate in any violence, partisans are more likely to shield their eyes when those associated with their own party perpetrate violence. Recent evidence further shows that partisans are more likely to regress to dehumanizing language toward members of the opposing party.[31] Anyone familiar with the historical antecedents of genocide understands the role dehumanization plays in justifying and propagating violence, oppression, and murder of those deemed subhuman.

Partisanship can even literally cost lives by distorting opinions about threat and danger. The most recent glaring example of this is the threat presented by the COVID-19 pandemic and the politically-motivated responses of both Democrats and Republicans. Under encouragement from political elites, many Republicans ignored the threat and failed to follow safety protocols that could have saved thousands of lives. At the height of the pandemic in July 2020, only 46 percent of Republicans identified the coronavirus as a major threat to the United States.[32] Furthermore, "counties that voted for Donald Trump over Hillary Clinton in 2016 exhibited 16 percent less physical distancing from March 9 to May 8, 2020" and that flaunting of health guidelines "in strongly pro-Trump counties . . . was associated with a 27 percent higher growth rate in COVID-19 infections."[33] Meanwhile, many politically-motivated Democrats blindly advocated for shutting down the economy and closing schools and institutions, regardless of economic and mental health consequences.

My purpose here is not to blame one side or the other. In fact, if your primary concern is which party gets blamed, you are definitely suffering from a mental illness. The coronavirus crisis was a complex problem without easy or perfect solutions. What I want to make clear through these examples is that partisanship compounded the problem, making the burden (and consequences) of the crisis worse by reinforcing our narrow-sighted perceptions, and making us even more blind to the weaknesses and limitations of our own perspectives. Too many Americans lost sight of the complex challenges at hand, preferring instead to use a deadly worldwide crisis to promote partisan sanctimony.

The negative outcomes of partisanship on our personal lives and society are far-reaching and pervasive. Yet, while most Americans may not link these problems to partisanship, they do sense that "there is something terribly wrong with this country."[34] In a 2019 survey, roughly 70 percent of Democrats, Republicans, and Independents claimed to recognize that America deals with disagreement in a destructive way.[35] When asked "How important is it for the United States to try to reduce divisiveness?" *92 percent* of Americans claimed it was important, with 65 percent saying it's "very important." While most Americans agree that political divisiveness is a serious problem, few connect it to partisanship. In fact, in the same survey mentioned above, less than a third of Americans "say destructive partisan disagreements and divisiveness have affected their personal lives." Although it seems that most Americans recognize that political hostility is a problem, too few of them acknowledge partisanship as the culprit.

Let's return to our earlier question: is partisanship really a mental disorder? Does it truly reach that level of destruction and dysfunction?

In search of an answer, I reviewed the evidence of partisanship's impact against the American Psychiatric Association's diagnostic criteria. Alcoholism shortens lives, interferes with productivity, and destroys social ties. Gambling addictions drain bank accounts, ruin families, and steal peace of mind. Partisanship kills relationships, interferes with economic activity, generates hatred, and in extreme cases, costs lives. In other words, partisanship meets the core criteria that classify mental illness—namely, that it causes unwanted distress and unhealthy problems in people's lives. Like other disorders, partisan leaning is not inherently excessive—one drink does not create an alcoholic—but the behavior can unfortunately devolve rapidly and without fanfare, all while leaving the afflicted to believe they're in total control of their decisions.

In the next chapter, I'll provide a model of "rational partisanship" that is productive, useful, and healthy. I'll then contrast that with the *irrational* form of partisanship that reaches the level of mental illness. Properly defining the parameters for partisanship as a mental illness requires comparison to a normal mental state, which is precisely the purpose of the next chapter.

Treatment: Airing Grievances

For this chapter, I simply want you to write down how partisanship has affected your life. Perhaps partisanship has strained your relationships with friends or family. Maybe you would like to talk about politics, but you stay silent because you're afraid people will get upset. Are you tired of getting angry, worried, and upset when you think about politics? Have you lost sleep thinking about what opposing politicians will do if they gain political power? Do you get frustrated that the government seems incapable of solving important problems?

Write down all your fears, concerns, and frustrations. Use this time to vent about partisanship and politics. Be as specific as you can. Name the friends and relatives you avoid, or those you wish you could talk to about politics. If you feel any amount of anger or frustration toward someone in your life because of their party identification, please list those people. We will return to that list in future chapters.

List the detailed ways you worry the other party will screw up your life. Describe the dystopia you fear will result from partisanship's death grip on this country. After you've completed this airing of grievances, move on to Chapter 3. Feel free to return to this section and add more things in the future. In fact, you will probably find this exercise makes you feel a lot better all on its own. I know it works for me!

CHAPTER 3

Two Forms of Partisanship

"Partisanship is our great curse. We too readily assume that everything has two sides and that it is our duty to be on one or the other."

— James Harvey Robinson

Every parent screws up their kid, it's just a question of how bad. My childhood was dysfunctional in unfortunately common ways, characterized by frequent exposure to domestic violence and economic insecurity. When the alcohol-fueled fights would start—usually late on Friday and Saturday nights—my response was to plug my ears, pretend I was asleep, and hope I survived the night. Although many days were non-violent, we were soul-crushingly poor and faced the daily threat of homelessness. Not surprisingly, I developed heightened anxiety in my childhood that carried over into adulthood. Even after escaping my external stressors, anxiety remained a problem in my life.

Once the human mind develops a habitual way of interacting with the world, it is very difficult to change. In my thirties, I learned I had developed a condition known as generalized anxiety disorder (GAD), which is characterized by restlessness, insomnia, irritability, and panic attacks. None of my childhood circumstances were my fault, but I nonetheless suffered the consequences for decades.

It is worth noting, however, that anxiety is not in itself a problem. The problem started when anxiety went too far and took too much precedence in the way I lived. Anxiety is actually a necessary and healthy part of living.[36] In fact, it is exactly the right response in some circumstances, and something you wouldn't want to live without. If you were about to accept a ride from a stranger, and felt a sense of anxiety, that would be your mind's way of telling you to rethink the decision. Anxiety helps alert us to danger and motivates us to find a better way forward.

As with most things in life, anxiety can go from something that started out good and beneficial, to a force that's draining and destructive. According to the Anxiety and Depression Association of America, approximately 18 percent of adults and 25 percent of adolescents in the United States suffer from an anxiety disorder. Unfortunately, only 37 percent of those suffering receive any kind of treatment. The sad reality is that too many people are living with anxiety in the driver's seat, instead of in the backseat where it belongs.

Why am I talking about anxiety in a book about partisanship? Well, anxiety is similar to partisanship in the way it functions. Party affiliation is *not* inherently unhealthy or destructive—in fact, it provides a variety of benefits. For one, party identification helps people make high-quality voting decisions when they lack a great deal of specific political information. Knowing a candidate's political party can help voters make predictions about what the candidate will do in office without the need to research their specific policy opinions or professional background. Furthermore, political parties themselves serve important roles in democracies by organizing political action among the public and elected leaders. Parties help legislative leaders form committees, structure votes, and deal with minor tasks that would otherwise be more complicated. The House of Representatives would find it nearly impossible to get anything done if it had 435 members who were completely unaffiliated with each other. Party affiliation is not all bad.

Just like anxiety, the extent to which partisanship is beneficial or harmful depends on whether it stems from rational or irrational beliefs and expectations. When anxiety stems from informed and rational beliefs about the world, it alerts us to things we *should* worry about, making it a necessary aid for our survival. But when anxiety stems from ignorant and irrational beliefs, it often leads to destructive behaviors such as crippling fear, social isolation, and substance abuse.[37]

Also similar to anxiety, partisanship benefits individuals and society when it is rooted in our rational beliefs about the world. But as I explained in Chapter 2, when partisanship results from unrealistic and irrational beliefs about society and members of the opposing party, it can have devastating consequences. Curing partisanship does not require us to eliminate all political parties or party identification, just as curing anxiety disorders does not require us to eliminate anxiety altogether. In order to address dysfunction, we need to address the underlying desires, feelings, and expectations that cause our beliefs to become irrational instead of rational.

What does it mean to hold political beliefs that are

rational? Simply put, rational beliefs are based on valid information about the world, and promote our life goals and interests. We are all humans capable of well-grounded and rational thought; of course, just because we're capable of rational thought doesn't mean we always use that power effectively. Heck, we can all remember some stupid ideas we believed or dangerous and idiotic things we did.

Other emotions and objectives get in the way of our ability to think clearly. Although we are capable of rationality, we far too often act in irrational ways, hold factually inaccurate beliefs, and make choices that aren't in our best interest, or the best interests of those we love. For example, alcoholics are rational people who are motivated to act as though slowly drinking themselves to death is a good idea. Many gamblers are motivated to believe they found a "system" that will beat the casino. Likewise, partisans are rational beings who are motivated to believe anything, and behave in any way that they think promotes their party's best interest. This motivation stems largely from an irrational fear of the opposing party.

The purpose of this chapter is to distinguish what I call "rational" partisanship from "irrational" partisanship. In brief, partisanship is rational when it stems from our worldview, values, principles, interests, and goals. Let me say that again: partisanship is supposed to result *from* our life goals and overarching principles. In the rational model, parties compete to give the people what they want, and voters support a party *only* in the moments when it addresses those concerns. Under the sway of irrational partisanship, this system is flipped upside down: party identity *influences* our values, morals, principles, and goals. In other words, an irrational partisan doesn't create their own beliefs and goals, but instead chooses whatever path most benefits their party, even when the party's goals conflict with the person's own best interests.

For rational partisans, their party affiliation is a consequence of their independent beliefs. Sadly, for far too many people, partisanship *determines* their political beliefs. As a result, partisans often end up voting against their own interests and supporting policies that violate their core values, principles, and life goals. Imagine living in a society where most people supported the party in power regardless of whether that party's goals aligned with the peoples' goals and values. This might remind you of an authoritarian regime like Hitler's rule in Germany, Mao Zedong's rule in China, or Stalin's rule in the Soviet Union. These authoritarian regimes collectively led to the deaths of more than 73 million people.

Now that we understand what's at stake when people get lost in irrational partisanship, let's explore the rational model of party identification and the key differences from its irrational form.

Rational Partisanship

How might a rational person choose a political party? Well, to answer that question, we must decide what we want from parties in a particular political system. What role should parties serve in a representative democracy such as the United States? Ideally, political parties allow for efficient law-making and governance in ways that promote the goals, values, and well-being of society as a whole. In other words, political parties are supposed to promote the public interest through government policy (or lack thereof). If parties are meant to represent the public interest, it is important to understand where those interests come from.

As we go through life, our minds create ways for us to understand how the world works. This constitutes our personal *worldviews*. Our worldviews represent our personal understanding of fundamental philosophical questions, such as the existence and role of God, free will, personal responsibility, justice, fairness, happiness, and the meaning of life—you know, the kind of stuff you only talk about with your friends when you're drunk or high.

Each person's worldview is informed by their individual culture, self-interest, family, religion, temperament, and general place in society. Importantly, we each have unique worldviews, because no two people can live the exact same life. As a result, diversions and disagreements are inevitable; we will never completely see the world in the same way or agree on everything. These interpersonal disagreements can cause anger, because we fail to remember that other people have lived different lives, have different personalities, and therefore interpret events in fundamentally different ways.

Our worldviews tie directly into our personal value systems. Our political *values* reflect our preferences for government action (or inaction). You can think of values as overarching desires that often compete and conflict with each other.

The five predominant political values are: Security, Opportunity, Freedom, Fairness, and Tranquility (SOFFT). A brief explanation of each value is provided below.

Security: The desire to protect yourself, and the people and things you care about, from harm.

Opportunity: The desire to provide yourself and others with the ability to thrive as human beings.

Freedom: The desire to allow people to live the way they want, even if you or others disagree with those pursuits.

Fairness: The desire to treat individuals equally, on grounds of justice and an even playing field.

Tranquility: The desire for comfort, peace, and harmony, knowing that other living things are not facing excessive mental or physical suffering. You could substitute 'conscience' for tranquility if you prefer.

Each of these is broad, and most of us desire each one to varying degrees, depending on our worldviews, temperaments, and unique situations. And sometimes these values (like all values) may come into conflict or modulate each other. For example, we all seek *security* from external threats, but also want *freedom* to do as we please. But we don't want others acting so freely that they can just rob and assault us anytime they want, because that would threaten our own sense of security. We also don't want to feel completely secure by demanding everyone else live exactly the way we want them to, because that would result in an oppressive lack of freedom. We also have a general desire for *opportunities* to create a good life, and we want rules and social systems to adhere to our sense of *fairness*. A desire for mental *tranquility*, or peace of mind, relates to our compassion for other living things and motivates us to care for and protect the things we love. The awareness that others are suffering or facing injustice disrupts our peace of mind. Laws are one way we seek to satisfy these values, even though our values inevitably conflict with one another.

Collectively, personal values guide the *principles* for how We the People ought to act and what rules governments ought to impose. Principles are general guidelines for behavior, such as: stealing is wrong, all races should be treated equally, every child should get a quality education, or the United States should promote peace around the world.

The key to understanding principles is that they should guide our decisions and policy preferences even when they lead to results we don't agree with. For example, if you believe every vote should count equally, you may oppose the Electoral College, even though its existence benefits candidates from your political party. Conversely, if you believe presidents should be required to have geographically diverse coalitions of voters, you may support the Electoral College, regardless of which party it benefits.

At times, you'll have to weigh your competing internal principles against one another, and you'll arrive at different verdicts depending on the circumstances. For example, your principles may support freedom of speech, but still allow the government to punish someone for shouting "I have a bomb!" on an airplane because you also believe that threats of violence and murder should be punished by the government. All values must have limits in order to be healthy. In this case, your value for free speech may reach its limit when someone threatens to murder hundreds of people.

By applying your values and principles to specific circumstances, you form the foundation for your policy preferences. Under rational partisanship, you'll then vote for candidates whom you believe will deliver policies and laws that align with your values and principles as much as possible. Remember, the purpose of government is to create and implement laws that ultimately promote the public interest. Political parties are institutions that help organize and mobilize common interests, so a large-scale society can more easily create widely beneficial government policies. As such, a political party is only useful to you if it actually promotes your interests better than any other party, or no party at all.

While some voters may ignore political parties entirely, most voters use party labels as a shortcut to help them choose the best candidates when they don't have a lot of specific information, since a candidate's party label can help us infer their stances on key issues and the future actions they may pursue. Party labels are especially useful for down-ballot races (such as those for mayor, state legislature, or district attorney) since most people lack sufficient information about candidates for those offices.

If you're critical of this shortcutting, simply ask yourself: Who are your state legislators right now? What are their positions on transportation funding or education reform? Chances are you have no idea! But you probably voted for them or their opponent based on the party label next to their name on your ballot. In an ideal world, all voters would always have complete and perfect information about every candidate and initiative, and the Chicago Cubs would win the World Series every year. Unfortunately, neither of those expectations are realistic.

Looking at party labels can be helpful when we lack sufficient information, but unfortunately, such shortcuts can also be dangerous if we use them incorrectly or rely on them too heavily.

Irrational Partisanship

In contrast to the rational model, an irrational partisan first identifies with a political party, then alters their voting decisions, issue preferences, principles, values, worldview, and even experiences to match whatever benefits the party. Under this model, there is no assurance that voters will make decisions that actually promote their own well-being, much less the well-being of their society. Instead, irrational partisans shape their beliefs and interpretations of the world to fit whatever the party thinks. They are not free-thinking, independent actors, but rather sheep who follow the lead of their party, regardless of the consequences for their lives, relationships, community, country, or even species.

How do irrational partisans select their party? Although many factors are involved, irrational partisans tend to select the party that they feel looks and acts the most like them.[38] For example, if someone is a white, male, evangelical Christian from a small town, he is likely to default to the Republican Party. Meanwhile, a Black female with a graduate degree, who was born in a big city, is likely to assume she belongs with the Democratic Party. Importantly, *perceptions* of the party's members matter much more than the actual membership. If you grew up in a Republican-affiliated household and your parents regularly criticized Democrats, you'll likely view the Republican party as morally or intellectually superior. In contrast, you may view Democrats as dumb, lazy, or otherwise inferior. I will discuss these partisan stereotypes more in the next chapter.

Once they've identified with a political party, irrational partisans feel motivated to always see that party in a positive and superior light. Because their party has become an identity, if the party is wrong, that means they must be wrong too! So, the party must remain justified in its actions at all costs in order to protect the partisan's self-image.

The more their party becomes part of their identity, the more *cognitive dissonance* partisans feel whenever they disagree with or question any choice made in the name of their party. Cognitive dissonance is the term used to describe the uncomfortable state of anxiety and stress people feel whenever they recognize that they simultaneously hold two conflicting opinions or beliefs. The human mind is motivated to eliminate and avoid this discomfort, and so it often leads people to rationalize the conflict away, or just ignore it entirely. As a result, the more someone believes their party is good, or that the other party is bad, the more their mind is motivated to actually see their party in a positive light. Since this happens on an unconscious level, partisans are not aware when it takes place and cannot easily stop it from happening. You could be an irrational partisan and not even realize how much it's damaging your relationships and hindering you from achieving your goals in life. When taken far enough, these individual realities can reach the level of dysfunctional mental illness.

There are at least three reasons why irrational partisanship is unhealthy and dangerous:

First, irrational partisanship makes people less likely

to support candidates and policies that promote their interests and goals, because partisanship increases the separation between actual and perceived reality. To some extent, there will always be a difference between what we perceive and how the world really is, but partisanship introduces a significant and consistent bias in our perceptions. The problem is that if we are motivated to believe our party is indeed promoting our interests, we are certainly more likely to reach that conclusion, even if the party is actually harming us. In this way, partisanship undermines the very usefulness of political parties, because it prevents us from accurately evaluating how well parties fulfill their duties. The desire to keep the other party out of power motivates partisans to see an alternative reality where their party's candidates do a great job, and the other party is incompetent and evil.

Moreover, irrational partisans will even believe that their lives are in better shape when their candidate is in office, compared to when the other party is in power. For example, following the 2016 presidential election, Trump voters reported higher subjective well-being and happiness, while Clinton voters reported lower subjective well-being six months after the election. Furthermore, the election of Donald Trump made Clinton voters believe that their lives were worse even in the months immediately following the election, when Barack Obama was *still president* and Trump had no official power.[39]

It's not healthy for our very sense of wellbeing and safety to be threatened every time there's an election, and partisanship is largely to blame. In 2019, 38 percent of Americans said that politics made them feel stressed, and that number increased to 68% just before the 2020 presidential election.[40] Studies also suggest that worrying about politics can result in loss of sleep and increased alcohol use.[41]

Second, partisanship also interferes with our ability to get along with each other. As I'll explain in Chapter 5, partisans come to feel that the other party is generally less trustworthy, more ignorant, and more apt toward evil intentions. Partisans also tend to believe the other party is more ideologically extreme and untrustworthy than their own.[42] For irrational partisans, conversations with friends and relatives often cause stress, because they find it difficult to understand how anyone could support the other party unless they were immoral or downright stupid. For example, a majority of Democrats believe most Republicans are racists and sexists.[43] If that's what you believe, it would certainly make it difficult to remain on positive terms with a friend or relative who is a Republican. Likewise, a Republican who believes Democrats are actively trying to destroy America would have a difficult time remaining on good terms with them.[44] If you firmly believe members of the other party are immoral and stupid people, you're under the grips of unhealthy irrational partisanship.

Third, partisanship promotes the weaponization of government, turning government into a tool of oppression rather than an instrument to promote the public good. Under the influence of irrational partisanship, governmental authority becomes an opportunity to suppress the minority party's voice. If partisanship guides principles (rather than the other way around), then *party* matters more than right and wrong. Imagine if party leaders began suppressing the vote of the opposing party in the name of the "greater interest." The same could be applied to freedom of speech, the press, or criminal procedures.

Would you stand by your independent principles, or would you side with your party? Too many partisans are likely to rationalize the oppressive action and embrace the party line, closing their eyes to its unethical nature and adopting the oppressive policy stances of their party leaders. If partisanship motivates you to support your party no matter what, you are likely to rationalize the oppression of the other party as an act of national interest, or to downplay it as not really a big deal. Of course, any action by the other party that you can conceivably classify as oppression of *your* rights would be the worst thing that has ever happened in the whole history of the world.

Under the rational partisanship model, your principles serve as an important check on your own party. Any party that violates the principles of too many of its voters would lose their support. But voters can keep political parties in check only when they live by stable principles and values that are grounded in independent thought, not partisan dogma. Once party affiliation becomes the source for a person's principles, values, and interests, those voters can no longer provide an effective check on their own party.

The principles of irrational partisans are guided by party and media elites, which can result in a powerful tidal wave of oppression. My friends, this really is how democracy ends—not in chaos, but in an orderly usurpation of power by groups that do not respect the perspectives and rights of those who disagree with them. Perhaps you believe democracy is overrated and wouldn't mind terribly if the other party didn't have much say in government. After all, they're just immoral fools who don't know what's good for them, right? Well, those given to irrationality in the other party feel the exact same way about you! I bet you would feel differently if the other party gained the majority and used the levers of power to suppress your voice, degrade your community, and take your property along with your rights.

If irrational partisanship is so dangerous to individuals and society, why would anyone choose it? That's like asking why someone would choose to be an alcoholic or compulsive gambler. A person does not become an alcoholic with their first sip of beer, nor does someone automatically transform into a compulsive gambler when placing their first bet. The woes of partisanship are sneaky and often develop slowly, in small steps. In the next three chapters, I'll explain the surprising history of how irrational partisanship became so pervasive in our current American culture.

This chapter has laid out two alternative models of partisanship: the rational and irrational models. In the rational model, party labels are simply a useful tool for making decisions when information is scarce. Rational partisans vote for whichever party best represents their personal principles and life goals. Importantly, rational partisans serve as a check on their parties because they are willing to remove their support if the party violates their principles or fails to promote their goals. A rational partisan would never utter the phrase, "It's my party, right or wrong." Rational partisanship creates more consistent personal behaviors that allow citizens to advance their life goals over the long term through government policy (or lack thereof).

Treatment: Establish Principles and Preferences

In order to practice rational partisanship, you must first establish your own goals, principles, and issue preferences. Without understanding what you want government to do, you won't be able to hold your party accountable or switch party allegiance when they fail to bring about the changes you desire. The purpose of this task is to help you better understand what you want from government.

Take some time to write down the political issues that are most important to you, and why they are important. What matters most in your life? Perhaps you want to have a successful career or start your own business. Maybe you have children and want them to grow up in a safe environment, get a good education, and lead a happy life. Or you may be content to sit on the couch, eat junk food, and watch television. What government policies would help you achieve this version of the good life? What current laws or programs are standing in the way? The key here is to identify the political issues that you care about most and articulate precisely why you care about those topics. Identifying why you care will help you prioritize these issues and select the ones that will best promote your idea of the good life, whatever that may be.

Once you have identified your most important issues, write down your preferred government policies for each one. What would you like the government to do, or to stop doing, regarding each issue? This doesn't need to be specific—just jot down your general preferences. For example, if you're concerned about climate change, you might want government to reduce global carbon emissions.

Perhaps abortion is an important issue, and you would like the government to ban it nationwide. Maybe gun control is an important issue, and you wish the government would impose stricter regulations on firearms, or conversely, you want a nationwide open-carry policy.

Write down as many issues and policies as you want; ideally, you'll have at least four issues and four corresponding policy preferences. Please don't skip this step, because we are going to return to these lists in future chapters. Without these lists you won't be able to complete those helpful exercises.

CHAPTER 4

How Partisanship Divides Americans

*"Nothing in life is to be feared, it is only to be understood.
Now is the time to understand more, so that we may fear
less."*

—Marie Curie

The Great Smoky Mountain National Park is only a few
hours' drive from my home, and my family and I travel
there frequently. If you've never been to the Smokies, I
highly recommend it. It's a beautiful mix of mountains,
rivers, waterfalls, and quirky Appalachian towns. One
morning I was hiking through the woods on the Tennessee
side of the park when I came upon a clearing. Just after
dawn, this meadow was nothing short of spectacular—
until all of a sudden, a very large creature lifted its head
above the tall grass, no more than fifty yards from where
I stood, and stared right at me. This animal probably
weighed several hundred pounds and stood a foot or two
taller than me. If it were aggressive, I would stand little
chance in a confrontation. What should I do? Should I
run? Play dead? Whip out my phone and take a picture?
Of course, my actions should depend on what type of
living thing it is, right?

Fortunately for me, the human mind is equipped to
handle this situation. Upon seeing the creature, my mind

immediately sought to classify it based on its physical characteristics. This process occurred so automatically that I wasn't even aware it was happening—I just did it. And as I did, the immediate shock I felt at unexpectedly seeing this large creature turned to delight: my mind recognized it as an elk, and I realized I had little to fear. My reaction would have been different if I had identified it as a bear, sasquatch, or rancor. Rapidly categorizing the animal based on group similarities and characteristics helped me make a quick decision about how to behave in that moment. Hypothetically, if the animal had been a bear, I certainly would not have stopped to question whether I was being unfairly prejudicial by assuming it's dangerous. After all, I had never met this bear before, so it might have been unfair of me to assume it was just as dangerous as other bears. The human mind naturally uses rough characteristics to group common things together in order to make quick, reliable-enough decisions about how we should behave. Granted, it's not always a perfect process, but it's much quicker and more productive than approaching every single object in the world with a completely blank slate.

Social Categorizations

Just as our brains work to quickly classify wildlife, when we meet new *people*, our minds automatically seek to categorize them based on their most obvious visual characteristics. Even if we don't intend to, our minds make quick judgments about others based on their height, weight, sex, hair, clothing, posture, attractiveness, facial expression, and yes, skin color. We use these physical characteristics to quickly categorize this new person so we can interact with them more effectively. This perfectly natural process is also the basis for some racism, sexism, ageism, and most forms of ignorant hatred. To be clear, the point of all this is not to justify racism or sexism, but to explain where they come from. Our ingrained mental processes, when left unchecked, can lead to some pretty horrific and despicable behavior. At the same time, these mental processes are an important part of how human minds work and they keep us safe.

We also automatically make inferences upon learning about people's other characteristics such as wealth, religion, ideology, party identification, and more. When I meet someone new, I absolutely dread the inevitable question of "What do you do?" Sometimes I say "Nothing," so they'll leave me alone. Admitting my horrible secret—that I'm a college professor—immediately causes some to assume I'm some arrogant intellectual. To be clear, I don't think I'm better than anyone else; I'm worse. Much, much, worse. Truth be told, almost none of the professors I've met think they are better than other people. If anything, they are overly critical of themselves and understate their self-worth. Yet, when people learn I'm a professor, they sometimes assume I'm arrogant, and interpret every action through that prism.

Although stereotypes like these can be fairly annoying, discriminatory, and often inaccurate, they are a useful part of the way our minds work. This ability to mentally categorize others into groups is critical to our survival because it helps us decide whom we can trust. Just as I categorized the elk, we instinctually categorize other humans because sometimes it helps us survive. If

I'm walking down a city street after dark, and a big man with a ski mask over his face jumps out from an alley, I won't stop and try to get to know him. Instead, I'll assume he can't be trusted and I'll either run or stand my ground, ready to fight. Similarly, our brains throw up red flags when we meet abusers, con artists, or other untrustworthy individuals—assuming we have a category of characteristics from past experiences that we identify in them. Rather than assessing each new person individually, our minds make guesses about who they are and how they'll behave based on the groups to which we believe they belong, and the beliefs we hold about those groups. What we really want to know, though, is the extent to which we should fear or trust this new individual.

When we classify people as "like us," we assume they are more predictable, and therefore, safer. All things equal, we tend to prefer predictable people over unpredictable people. In contrast, when we perceive someone as very different, we feel more uneasy about their motivations and potential behaviors. We feel like we don't understand them as well. We classify people we perceive as "like us" as part of our in-group, while everyone else belongs to out-groups. This applies as much to political groups as any other. Your categorizing brain—which exists to keep you alive—can work against you by breeding political group hatred and fear.

This relates to expressions of tribalism, where members of one group (such as a tribe, gang, fraternity, or cult) wear similar colors, clothes, or tattoos in order to more easily identify who is on their side and who is with an opposing group. With this is mind, it's easy to see how skin color remains such an easy categorization signal—despite its complete uselessness in predicting behavior from a genetic standpoint—simply because it is a prominent visual characteristic. The same is true of sex, height, weight, and attractiveness, which is why those characteristics are so often the basis for prejudice, exclusion, and degradation. Although our minds automatically judge appearances, the problem occurs when our judgments also affect the conclusions we draw about each individual's character.

For a moment, I want you to use your imagination and be completely honest with yourself. Picture a white man standing six feet tall, with jeans, a t-shirt, and dark hair. On a scale of 0-100, I would like you to think of a number that represents how you feel about this person, with 0 being very negative and 100 meaning very positive. Now, what if I told you this man was Black instead of white? How would you rate him now? What if I told you he was a Republican? Still being honest with yourself, how do you feel about him now? What changed? Upon learning that this man was Black, your mind likely gave him characteristics of other Black people based on your experiences and knowledge.

Attributing these group characteristics to the individual may have made you more or less favorable toward this person. Likewise, learning that this man was a Republican probably changed your perceptions of him in either a positive or negative direction, depending on your perceptions of and experiences with other Republicans. Ask yourself this: which characteristic had a larger effect on your feelings toward this person? My guess is that it was his party identification, not his race, that changed your feelings the most. If your learning of his partisanship changed your rating substantially, then you may be living under heavy partisan dysfunction than you realize. The stronger your gut reaction to this character's party identification, whether positive or negative, the more likely it is that you have a problem. If this is news to you, I'm sorry I had to be the one to deliver this unfortunate diagnosis.

But you can heal yourself. Just keep reading.

Political Isolation

Although party identification has become a very prominent social identity in America today, this wasn't always the case. For most of the twentieth century, party affiliation stretched beyond the borders of other social divides. There were conservative Democrats in the South and liberal Republicans in the North.[45] Most importantly, Republicans and Democrats used to live amongst each other and interact more often than they do today.[46] But then, late in the twentieth century, the United States went through a "Big Sort," where the social groups identifying with each political party fundamentally changed.[47] This sorting happened for a variety of reasons, including increased geographic mobility, religious activism, social movements, and Party-issue alignment.[48] Over time, many southern conservative Democrats became solidly Republican, while many northern Republicans became firm Democrats.[49] Meanwhile, Evangelical Christians moved largely behind the Republican Party. Finally, the largest growing ethnic group at the time, Hispanics, transitioned from a roughly equal split in party identification to more Democratic-leaning (now split roughly 70-30).

As a result of this Big Sort, it's now much easier for

people to identify which party (supposedly) represents people like them. Just by looking at somebody and learning where they live and what other beliefs they hold, it's fairly easy to place them automatically "where they belong." An important consequence of this social sorting is that people stopped living around members of different parties, which made the other party seem even more foreign and distant. Republicans increasingly made their home in rural areas, while Democrats increasingly moved to urban homes. Even now when Democrats and Republicans reside in the same regions, they often live away from each other in segmented communities, among others just like them.[50] Though they may pass people with different perspectives, experiences, and political ideas on their way to work, the people they interact with in their neighborhoods, schools, churches, and community organizations generally hold the same political beliefs they do. For a visual representation of this geographic segregation and to see how it affects your city, check out the interactive map at projects. fivethirtyeight.com/republicans-democrats-cities/.

This geographic sorting acts as an incubator for more of the same, making it more likely that Democrats and Republicans will develop their ideas predominantly around people exactly like them.[51] While in the past Democrats and Republicans mingled together in schools, community events, and churches, they now are more likely to live in political enclaves where they are mostly surrounded by like-minded partisans. During the 2020 presidential election, very few Democrats or Republicans claimed to have "more than a few" (if any) friends supporting the other party.[52]

What all of this illustrates is a worrisome trend:

partisanship is no longer just a useful heuristic; it's now a prominent social identity. Partisans now perceive their party as an in-group and the other party as an out-group. Politics is no longer about my thoughts and perspectives; it's now about us and them, "one of us" or "one of them."[53]

Social identity theory argues that an individual may feel they belong to any number of categories, whether they identify as a "female," "Cubs fan," "Black," "Italian," "bisexual," or "entrepreneur." These self-identifications can become more or less prominent in a person over time and in different circumstances. When a particular social identity is given more weight or focus for whatever reason, humans intrinsically seek to elevate the status of that group, regardless of whether there's any personal benefit in doing so. For example, if race is made more salient, whites are less likely to support social welfare policies because they (incorrectly) believe Black people will be the primary beneficiaries.[54] In fact, most welfare recipients are white, but the belief that it primarily benefits Blacks motivates some whites to oppose those subsidies.[55] In short, the more strongly someone identifies with a group, the more they will seek to discriminate against out-groups.

The Partisan Divide Is an Illusion

The problem with the narrative of partisan division is that it largely ignores other important similarities and differences between individuals across society. Democrats and Republicans are *not* fundamentally different people; it is only when we focus on political affiliations that the partisan divide actually divides us. Members of both parties sit in prisons and pews. There are rich Democrats and poor Republicans, single Republicans and married Democrats. There are an infinite number of ways to slice and dice the diversities and similarities among members of a society. So why do we spend so much time looking at partisanship, rather than other, more important similarities? The short answer is that politicians and the media brainwash us to believe it's important. This is precisely how partisanship can lead us to act in ways that harm our own welfare. If you are a poor person who identifies firmly with one political party, your party may enact policies that actually leave you worse off—and they do it by means of your support! It is better to make voting decisions by looking at each policy on a case-by-case basis, but partisanship prevents us from rationally and objectively considering the full scope of public policy consequences. Partisans have oversimplified *themselves* to fit into a party-defined box. As a result, they inevitably support policies that harm them, while protesting laws that would actually benefit their lives.

Furthermore, partisans hold biased misperceptions of members of the opposing party. Both parties believe the other party is filled with people who are not like them and who are fundamentally different in important ways. For example, in a 2015 survey, Republicans estimated that over a third (36 percent) of Democrats were Atheist or Agnostic, but only 9 percent of Democrats actually identify as such. Republicans also believed that 46 percent of Democrats were Black (actual: 24 percent), 38 percent were lesbian, gay or bisexual (actual: 6 percent), and 44 percent were Union members (actual: 11 percent). Conversely, Democrats overestimated the number of Republicans who were 65 and older (44 percent vs. 21

percent) and believed that 44 percent earned more than $250,000 a year, when only 2 percent actually made that much.[56] These misperceptions have important implications for partisans' perceptions of the other party's motivations. If Democrats believe Republicans are richer than they actually are, they are more likely to attribute Republican positions on tax policy to selfish greed rather than principled opposition to wealth redistribution.

Partisans also misperceive the issue positions of opposing partisans. Specifically, they tend to believe members of the opposing party hold more extreme opinions about political issues than they actually do. An interesting survey by the group "More In Common" asked Americans to estimate how many Democrats and Republicans hold extreme views. Overall, Americans believed that 55 percent of members of the other party held extreme views. When the same survey measured the political views of partisans, less than a third (30 percent) actually held extreme opinions.[57] And worse: the groups most likely to overestimate the extremeness of the other party are those who are most active and engaged in the political system. That is to say, the people who are most consequential to the political system—because they donate and vote consistently—are the most wrong about the extremeness of the other party. Although the news media and party elites constantly tell us with conviction that Democrats and Republicans are fundamentally different people, they are actually much more similar, and more reasonable, than we think.

The idea that America is divided into two distinctly defined partisan tribes is an illusion that politicians and the news media perpetuate for *their* personal gain. In fact,

Democrats and Republicans contain subgroups that have a lot in common with each other. The problem is that we act as though partisanship represents a truly meaningful difference between Americans (guess what, it doesn't!).

Make no mistake, I am certainly not arguing that we are all exactly the same. There are important differences in American society that lead us to have fundamentally different interests and perspectives on specific public policies, and that's why rational partisanship can be helpful. Americans are diverse in their cultures, perspectives, classes, races, interests, and ambitions. Partisanship overlaps some of those things and translates into voting behavior, but the idea that Republicans and Democrats are fundamentally different people—or that all Republicans or all Democrats are essentially the same—is absolutely an illusion. When we let go of this false Democratic-Republican divided lens and recognize the real social groups involved in a political issue, and their unique priorities and needs, we can make more progress. Those who hold more wealth in society have interests that are distinct from those of poor people, and we should not gloss over that fact. For good reason, Black people are more afraid of the police than white people, and women are more afraid of sexual assault than men. The same is true for other social differences based on countless other individual circumstances.

What I am arguing is that people who affiliate as a Democrat or Republican share many important interests and similarities, but these are often overlooked because of partisanship. This illusory difference in identity obscures much more important individual circumstances that should determine where we stand on specific political issues. Instead, we see another person under the label of "Democrat" or "Republican" and ignore the countless ways we are similar in our goals, desires, families, and social situations. Likewise, we often incorrectly believe others in our party share the same underlying interests and goals. These misperceptions cause partisans to oppose policies that would help them, while supporting laws that harm their lives.

Bridging the Gap

A few years ago, a friend from graduate school came to visit. Just days before the visit, we had fallen into a political disagreement on social media. For the first few hours of the visit, I only looked at him through the prism of our political differences. How could he believe what he did? *He's wrong and he needs to know it*, I thought.

But after a while it dawned on me that he was really struggling with some problems in his life. His marriage was falling apart, and he was worried about how a divorce might affect his daughter, whom he loved very much. Our political differences immediately receded into the background and I returned to being his compassionate, sympathetic, and caring friend. Our political differences were minor compared to everything we shared in common, which is what made us good friends in the first place. It was only when I focused on politics that we seemed so different—but that is such a small part of our friendship.

Want to be part of the solution to our country's growing hatred? Stop focusing on the one way people in the other party are different from you, and start considering all the things you have in common with those humans on the other side. Research suggests that focusing on any non-political similarities can decrease political hostility. For example, one study found that increasing the prominence of national identity as American citizens can reduce emotional responses to differences.[58] In other words, when disagreeing partisans focus on their shared national identity, they feel less negative toward one another. The same study also found that partisans tend to become more positive toward opposing partisans after learning that they root for the same sports teams. Something as small and insignificant as the team you root for can de-escalate partisan anger and hostility!

There are countless life concerns that we already share with individuals in the opposing party—education, religion, community interests, ambitions, parenting, music, even dog or cat ownership. When we focus on that one difference (party affiliation), we are more inclined to automatically dislike and distrust members of the other party. But when we focus on other, arguably more important similarities, we are more likely to recognize our shared humanity and better understand the individual experiences and perspectives of opposing partisans. The next time you begin to feel animosity or anger toward an opposing partisan, remember that the best way forward is to find something you might agree on and focus the conversation on that, at least for the time being.

Treatment: Identify Commonalities

Return to the list of people you know in the other party, or anyone you would like to discuss politics with, but disagreement stands in the way. For each of those people, list nonpolitical things that you have in common. Based on what you know about them, what do you think are the most important things in their life?

If it's not too much trouble, you could ask them in person or through social media. Simply say, "I'm surveying my friends and family to find out what matters most to them in their daily lives. What are your goals, biggest daily concerns, and hobbies?" If they mention anything political, that's fine, but you don't need to mention politics at all.

The point of this exercise is to identify the things you have in common, and to demonstrate that those commonalities are often the things that matter most in life. Hopefully, this exercise will help you see your friends and relatives as more complete human beings, and not simply as Democrats or Republicans.

CHAPTER 5

Partisan Hatred

"Ignorance leads to fear, fear leads to hate, and hate leads to violence."

– Averroës

History is filled with examples of political hostility ending in oppression, violence, and death. A few recent examples are particularly noteworthy.

On January 6, 2021, hundreds of people stormed the United States Capitol building. Members of Congress were sent running for safety. Security tried to ward off intruders while some members of the crowd severely beat on-site police officers. The invasion killed five people, including one police officer, and sent another to the hospital. Earlier, just before the 2020 election, thirteen people attempted to kidnap the governor of Michigan. According to Michigan law enforcement, the kidnapping was part of a broader conspiracy to "instigate a civil war."[59] There are also many recent examples of political violence between citizens. In August 2020, a man in Portland, Oregon, shot another man over a political dispute. During a protest, a 17-year-old crossed state lines with an automatic weapon and killed two people. An argument over a political sign posted in someone's yard ended with a woman being shot to death.[60] Rioters in 2020 vandalized private property and set fires to small businesses, some of which were owned by members of their own community.[61] These violent acts were carried out by liberals and conservatives, Democrats and Republicans.

Politically motivated violence is not isolated to a few deranged outcasts. In a survey I conducted just before the 2020 election, over one thousand Americans were asked, "How often do you feel like people in the other party just deserve to be slapped?" Less than a quarter (22 percent) of Americans said "never," with an equal number (23 percent) saying "sometimes," while more than half said either "about half the time" (20 percent), "most of the time" (20 percent) or "always" (15 percent). That's right, over three-quarters of Americans said that complete strangers in the other party need to be slapped, at least sometimes. A survey conducted in 2019 found that "about one in five Americans with a strong political affiliation say they are quite willing to endorse violence if the other party wins the presidency."[62]

How does political disagreement come to this? What makes otherwise ordinary people resort to lawlessness, violence, and murder? In the previous chapter, I explained how minimal contact with opposing partisans makes it difficult to acknowledge our similarities. Politically isolated partisans are unable to understand the motives—or predict the behavior—of people in the other party. The reason for this is their lack of contact with people who belong to the other party. People in their party generally share their interests, and see the world as they do, so it makes sense to identify with them. This is not necessarily a bad thing, and certainly not pathological to the level of mental illness.

It is perfectly reasonable to connect with others in

your community, with whom you have much in common, without disliking or fearing those who live differently than you. Furthermore, feelings of solidarity and connectedness with a social in-group can be a great thing when channeled to positive ends. When people feel a shared identity with others, it can motivate altruistic acts, such as donating to charities that benefit the less fortunate who are of a similar race, religion, or part of their local community. Noticing that other people have different characteristics does not automatically generate anger, contempt, or fear.

Unfortunately, partisanship *does* cause hostility between members of opposing parties. In fact, research suggests that partisans are more motivated by negative partisanship than they are by any affinity for members of their party.[63] This means that partisanship is better understood as a fear of the out-party than an enthusiasm or love for the in-party. This 'negative partisanship' serves as the strongest motivation for political activity.[64]

So why does partisanship cause political hostility, and what can we do about it? Let's start with echo chambers.

Partisan Echo Chambers

The world is an uncertain place. We face many decisions in our daily lives where we lack information and expertise. In situations where we acknowledge that we have insufficient expertise, we look to others who are more informed to help us make good decisions. There is no way we could know everything about every topic, so we rely on others for their knowledge in particular areas. If we were unable to trust others in this way, we'd never be able to build such incredible civilizations. We ask doctors for health advice, mechanics for car advice, and brokers for investing advice. Want the perfect wine with your meal? Ask a sommelier. (Or just get whatever wine you want.) You get the point! When you know you lack expertise in an area, you look to experts for insight.

Well, the same is true when it comes to politics. To help us understand what's going on politically, we seek out political elites who are knowledgeable about public affairs. Such individuals can include elected officials, policy experts, media commentators, and even politically-informed acquaintances. A political elite can be anyone who gets attention from a large number of people who trust their expertise on politics.

The most powerful political elites fall into two categories: 1) those who garner the most media attention, and 2) those who have influence over the ideas of the first group. Political elites tend to get more media attention when they hold a position of power (e.g., President, Speaker of the House), or when they say controversial things (e.g., Ann Coulter and Bill Maher). There are also media personalities, such as Sean Hannity, Rachel Maddow, or Erik Erickson, whose power stems from both the size of their audiences and the types of people they inform. Media personalities can have a small audience, but still have a large effect on the national dialogue if the particular people in their audience act as opinion leaders in their social networks.

Of course, the *perception* of expertise is all that matters here—not actual expertise. As long as people think you know what you're talking about, they will find your arguments more persuasive, regardless of how much you actually know. Most people have low levels of factual information about political policy issues and events, so they trust political elites to help them understand which policies they should support, how to interpret political events, and whom to vote for in elections. There is nothing inherently wrong with turning to political elites for help in understanding the political world. People trust political elites to clarify political events and frame political issues around potentially relevant values. Elites will "frame" an issue (such as gun control, education, immigration, etc.) when they emphasize one value or set of considerations in their discussions, while ignoring others.

In Chapter 2, I discussed the five main political values (Security, Opportunity, Freedom, Fairness, and Tranquility). Almost every political issue involves tradeoffs between these ideals, and almost every person holds each of these values to some degree. Of course, whether a value applies to a particular political issue depends on the individual and situational context.

Nonetheless, most of us can relate to these values to some extent. For example, gun control can be framed as a 2nd amendment issue (freedom), or as a public safety issue (security). Similarly, the debate over free college education can be framed as a question of *opportunity* for young people, especially those who come from poor families, or as a question of *fairness* for those who foot the bill for something that doesn't directly benefit them. Both values are at play here, and most people want both things: to provide opportunity and to avoid paying taxes with no personal benefit. If we remember both values at once, we correctly see that the question of education spending is a tradeoff between two competing values that we each hold. In contrast, if we only listen to our party's elites talk about the issue, it would seem as though there is only one value that matters in the discussion, and therefore anyone disagreeing with our party's policy is simply lacking in values and intelligence. As I will discuss later, the act of focusing on only one value while ignoring others is an error known as *polarized thinking*.

Why don't political elites provide both frames? Because they have absolutely no incentive to explain the other side's point of view. Instead, political elites have every reason to provide strong arguments for their preferred policies, and weak arguments for the opposing party. Elected officials want you to show up to vote (for them), donate to their campaigns, and get others to vote for them too. Media personalities want a large audience that keeps coming back—which boosts their ratings and allows their employers to charge more for advertising space. And guess what most effectively captures your attention? *Fear and division.*

Elected officials and media personalities want to turn you into a political activist who fears the other party so much that you donate your money, volunteer in their campaigns, and obsessively watch cable television news. Ask yourself this question: which of the following people is more likely to vote, donate money, and frequently tune into Fox News or MSNBC: someone who understands the arguments of both sides but slightly prefers their party, or someone who thinks the world will end if the other party gains an ounce of credibility? Political elites are fully incentivized to make you fear the other party gaining political power because that fear makes you act in ways that benefit them. In short, they are manipulating you to advance their careers and line their pockets!

There is a self-reinforcing feedback loop that occurs here as well. Increasingly extreme voters elect extreme candidates, and then those candidates create more extreme voters. First, party primaries incentivize candidates to take extreme positions to distinguish themselves from their in-party opponents and appeal to activist partisan voters. Then, once they've gotten the nomination, even more moderate partisans accept their extreme policies. Why? Because of one-sided framing by party elites, and that pesky cognitive dissonance their brains want them to avoid. In other words, partisans are inadvertently moved to adopt the frames of their more extreme party nominees during elections because they only trust their party's motives and strongly distrust the motives of the other party.[65] This is precisely how partisanship can begin to take hold as a mental illness.

The truth of the matter is that political elites have a personal incentive to make you fear the other party. And how do they successfully do that? They provide the strongest arguments in support of their own issue positions while providing pathetic arguments for the opposing side. While this at least helps their followers understand one argument or interpretation, it also implies that the issue revolves around only one political value. As a result, partisans come to believe that members of the other party simply do not care at all about the same values they do. But in reality, opposing partisans are just thinking about *different* values.

Consider the earlier example of spending on public education. While the Democrats connect free education to equality of opportunity, Republicans link it to government inefficiency. When partisans only listen to their own party, they end up believing that the opposing party doesn't hold the same values they do. Democrats come to believe that Republicans must not care about providing opportunities to poor children; likewise, Republicans come to believe that Democrats don't care about wasteful government spending ("tax-and-spend liberals"). Neither is true! Do you really believe Republicans oppose opportunity for poor children? Or that Democrats want the government to waste money?

If you are nodding your head 'yes' right now, you really need to keep reading.

The Terrifying Straw Man

Political elites also understand that people naturally want to know why others disagree with them. In my experience as an educator on politics and government, I have learned that even the most partisan students desire some explanation for why the other side of any debate holds the position they do.

When someone disagrees with us, it grabs our attention until we find some satisfying explanation. Perhaps our curiosity results from our underlying insecurity about our own opinions. Regardless of the motivation, this curiosity is a good thing. We should be skeptical of the absolute correctness of our political beliefs. It's good that we're not content to merely learn the arguments for one position, but that we instinctively crave at least some explanation for why others hold a different point of view.

Unfortunately for partisans, the political elites of their party are more than happy to serve up misleading and biased answers. They present "straw man" arguments that are logically weak and held up by dubious factual evidence. Most political elites are too smart to present completely absurd arguments. Instead, they often provide a semi-plausible explanation for the opinions of the other party—one that is just reasonable enough to satisfy the curiosity of their followers, but without yielding any credibility or validity to the other side. These explanations usually point to some intellectual or moral defect in members of the opposition.

For example, Democrats may claim that Republicans oppose welfare spending because they lack empathy for poor people. Meanwhile, Republicans typically attribute Democrats' support of welfare services to a lack of work ethic. Similarly, any time taxes come up (which is all the time), Democrats tend to accuse Republicans of wanting to hoard money among the wealthy. On the other side, Republicans often accuse Democrats of socialist redistribution of wealth from the working middle class to the poor. In other words, Republicans don't care about poor people while Democrats are extreme socialists. Political elites paint this civil disagreement as war between the two parties. Their party is the protagonist, fighting for justice, motivated by altruistic intent, and supported by unquestionable fact. This hero party is fighting against the antagonist, who is darkly motivated by self-interest and hatred and is too stupid to see or understand the truth.

Political elites also misrepresent the moral motivations of opposing partisans. Most commonly, political elites try to de-legitimize the opposition's stances and behavior by claiming they're simply playing "politics," or that they're trying to appease the extreme fringes of the party. In making such claims, the elites are suggesting that the opposing views are not only wrong, but fundamentally illegitimate and therefore dangerous. It is far easier to paint the other side as ideologically extreme than it is to confront the actual values motivating their behavior.

Though the absurdity of this logic may seem apparent, partisans who already see the other party as foreign and different will happily accept these explanations. After all, partisans increasingly segregate their daily lives into enclaves, where they get news from self-reinforcing sources and develop their ideas in incubators of more of the same. Since they're unlikely to have much contact with opposing partisans, they have a difficult time understanding and relating to members of the other group. Almost everyone in their family, church, community, and social networks reflect back to them the same ideas they already hold, so it's difficult to understand how anyone could disagree. And now their political elites, who are trusted because they're "like them," paint this picture of good versus evil. It's no wonder partisans buy into it and come to view the other party as ignorant, evil, and a grave threat to the nation.

As Lee Drutman puts it:

> To the political left, Donald Trump is un-American: His xenophobic, racist rhetoric stands in opposition to the true American vision of tolerance. It's an affront to our nation of immigrants, a country in which equality is written into our founding documents. Any Republican who supports or voted for him is guilty by association. To the political right, it's the Democrats who are un-American. They denigrate our founding as a [freedom-centered] nation and want to [communize] everything. They want to sacrifice our sovereignty to globalist institutions under the guise of invented problems like global

warming and to undermine our exceptional heritage by opening our borders [without discretion]. There is only one "real America" and it doesn't include the coasts or cities where many Democrats live.[66]

Of course, it also helps that these portraits depict members of your own party as the heroes and the other party as the villain. By idealizing my party as more intelligent and righteous than the other side, I feel a pleasant boost in my self-concept. This feeling of superiority creates an unconscious incentive to passively accept this flattering portrait of the political landscape, no matter how false the representation. This cycle is self-reinforcing because it makes its participants happier with themselves, which motivates them to ignore any evidence to the contrary. People are also more likely to automatically resist competing ideas when they face a symbolic threat to their party's righteousness. In other words, partisans develop knee-jerk hostility toward the other party in order to protect their own self-esteem.[67]

This magnificent setup produces one result: group-on-group anger, fear, and hatred. Partisans begin with the feeling that opposing partisans are fundamentally different from them. Then, they hear their political leaders, who should be more knowledgeable on the subject, explain that members of the other party are driven by selfishness, extreme ideology, ignorance, and otherwise illegitimate motivations. As a result, partisans develop ever-deepening anger and hostility toward those who continue to identify with the opposing party. How could they not? The other party supports laws that will affect everyone's lives, but for completely selfish and narrow-minded reasons! It's impossible to talk with them because they seem incapable of seeing the truth. In order to avoid this fruitless frustration, partisans simply avoid all contact with opposing partisans, which often leads to lost friendships and family estrangement. And since opposing partisans are fundamentally corrupt in their thinking and reasoning, it also makes sense to avoid pursuing any future relations with them.

This is how partisanship begins its life-destroying consequences for you and those you care about.

Dehumanization, Oppression, and Violence

Partisanship can also result in discrimination and oppression against members of the opposing party. If the thoughts, perspectives, and voting decisions of the other party are not legitimate, then naturally, we are justified in discriminating against them and suppressing their vote and speech. After all, they've proven themselves too stupid to vote for the right candidates, so it's probably best if they just don't vote at all.

I'm willing to bet many of you have had this very thought at one point or another—"It wouldn't be so bad if the other side just didn't show up on Election Day."

You can see how this seemingly innocent thought—a joke even—can lead to real support for policies that make it more difficult for the other party to be heard, share their views, and even vote. Everyone says they believe in freedom of speech, but when the other side is "fundamentally corrupted," society won't lose much if some modest restraints are put in place to curtail their freedom of speech and expression—right? Why should we bend over backward so they can voice their opinions, when their views are illegitimate? I hope you see where all of this leads: goodbye free speech, free press, and universal voting rights.

If you believe that it's perfectly fine to restrict the rights and freedoms of those whose perspectives you think are illegitimate, take a moment to consider how you would feel if your rights and freedoms were restricted with that same reasoning. When we allow this attitude to take hold, then whichever party happens to have power will act to restrict the rights of those who oppose them because they believe the opposition's opinions are illegitimate. This is precisely why governing principles that extend dignity to all humans—even those you disagree with—are so important.

That said, I suppose if we are forced to choose, it may be better to label opposing partisans as "ignorant" rather than "morally deficient." If we believe that they're simply ignorant, we may feel pity and try to help them understand the truth. The more dangerous belief is that opposing partisans are morally devoid—that's the real road to dehumanization, and it's how violence and oppression are often justified. It's distressing to note that recent research shows partisans are willing to dehumanize their neighbors and other fellow Americans who happen to identify with the opposing party. If this doesn't scare you, it should.

When you look back on history, you'll find that some of the most horrendous acts of political oppression, violence, and genocide were preceded by the rise of dehumanizing language. The Nazis engaged in systematic propaganda that labeled Jews as rats, while the Hutus called the

Tutsis cockroaches prior to the Rwanda genocide.[68] Communist propaganda labeled enemies as insects, lice, and bloodsuckers. Why engage in dehumanization? Because people are more willing to accept horrendous acts of violence and oppression against people they don't see as fully human. What do you do with vermin, pests, and infestation? You exterminate them.

Perhaps you think I'm overreacting, that this could never happen in America, because we're a democracy. Do you mean the same democracy that enslaved and lynched people because of their skin color? The same democracy that, less than one hundred years ago, put American citizens in camps because they happened to be of Japanese descent? And let me remind you that Germany was a democracy before a divisive speaker came along and divided them against specific groups based on arbitrary characteristics. If you think genocide and oppression can't happen here, history suggests you are dead wrong.

Research on today's partisans in the US gives an alarming indication that partisanship pushes us beyond innocent avoidance of the opposition, and into a state where we actually see the other side as less human. That point is worth repeating: Partisanship converts ordinary citizens into Democrats and Republicans who are unable to recognize the humanity in opposing partisans or even consider them worthy of basic human dignity and respect. This is the kind of revelation that should scare all Americans. It points to the danger of political authorities and influencers who exploit partisan conflict for their political and financial benefit.

To examine this link between partisanship and dehumanization, I'll point to two separate studies. In one study, Dr. Erin Cassese used data from two surveys during the 2016 presidential election to show that "partisans dehumanize their political opponents in both subtle and blatant ways." Furthermore, when partisans engage in dehumanization, they "prefer greater [relational] distance from their political opponents, which is indicative of reduced interpersonal tolerance."[69] In other words, partisanship decreases our tolerance of the opposing party (and those associated with it), as well as our desire to have any contact with them. Avoiding contact with opposing partisans makes us more likely to dehumanize them. Inter-group contact can reduce prejudice and increase tolerance, but it requires that we actually talk with people who see and think differently than we do. In another article, appropriately titled "Party Animals," the authors went further by employing both survey and experimental data in order to examine causation.[70] They found that strong party affiliation caused a willingness to accept dehumanizing portrayals of the opposing party. Specifically, they found an attitude of dehumanization was most common among those with the highest levels of animosity toward opposing partisans.

Partisanship is a mental disorder that, carried out to its end, erupts into violence. Dehumanization is a noteworthy step on this path toward political violence and oppression because it reduces empathy for the humans who associate with the disliked group. Most of us don't think much when we exterminate rats, roaches, or ants, but we feel much more empathy for our fellow humans. Humans are us. If violence is acceptable against any human, then what's to stop it from making its way to you?

The us/them narrative provided by partisanship solves

that problem: they are less than human; we are nothing like them. We are better than that. The illusory divide of partisanship distorts our perspective and makes us feel that other humans are less worthy of basic human respect. As we discussed earlier, political elites are motivated to use inflammatory language to stir up partisan animosity because it helps them gain attention and rile their listeners into action.

Neither side is innocent in this. Republican President Donald Trump frequently used dehumanizing language when criticizing leaders in the Democratic Party, referring to Democrats in Congress as "dogs," "crazy," "sick," and "savages."[71] Meanwhile, "liberals and Democrats, believing that their equality agenda is right and just [i.e. superior], increasingly cast those who oppose it in very negative terms like 'racist' and 'sexist.'"[72] While it may be politically convenient to demonize the opposing party, this lazy choice has longer-term consequences for our country's health.

Constantly calling the opposing party stupid, racist, sick, homophobic, immoral, or dishonest deteriorates the conversation and sends a signal that we are irreconcilable, that America is divided into good and evil, where the other party represents only irreparably contaminated human beings. Those who accept characterizations that demonize the other party are feeding a monster that's bigger than them—one that can (and, if we don't stop feeding it, *will*) grow beyond control, beyond what was ever intended. And all who are complicit in this self-satisfying behavior will be responsible for the havoc it wreaks and the lives it destroys.

I've seen this reckless disregard for the lives of opposing

partisans in my many of own personal discussions with both Democrats and Republicans. Just after Donald Trump won the 2016 Presidential election, I overheard someone say they wished "somebody would shoot that mother******!" Another time, I was talking about politics with a complete stranger at a bar when he confessed that he "would love someone to take a shotgun to" Hillary Clinton and Nancy Pelosi. Many others have said the world would be better if Democrats just disappeared. When President Trump was diagnosed with COVID-19, some of my Democratic friends quietly expressed their hope that he would refuse treatment and die.

These are just a few examples of the callousness I have encountered, but I'm willing to bet they are fairly common in other people's conversations as well. Although these pronouncements are often unexpected, shocking, and frightening—especially when coming from a stranger you were just making small talk with—there is an easy way to respond by appealing to their better natures. Simply saying "I don't wish harm on anyone," or "well, I don't think violence is the answer" will usually do the trick. Deep down most people understand that violence is wrong, and will usually take it back or say it was a joke when you calmly fail to reciprocate. If they insist that violence is the only answer, you may want to find a polite reason to leave as soon as possible!

Resisting Polarized Thinking

How can we fix this problem? Partisans see the world as divided into clear-cut right and wrong. This perspective is called "dichotomous (or polarized) thinking," when people believe that political issues are simply either-or problems.[73] That is, when we engage in polarized thinking, we take a complex political problem and treat it as though its solution is 'this or that,' black and white, right vs. wrong, good vs. evil. There is no middle ground or third option.

The two-party duopoly in the US only exacerbates this polarized approach to complex challenges. Many Democrats and Republicans strictly align with most or all of their party's official policy stances. As a result, political issues are treated more broadly as choices between one or the other, when in fact issues are multifaceted and involve numerous political values, interests, and complex causal relationships that no one fully understands.

Polarized thinking is attractive because it simplifies political issues, and politics in general. Take immigration, for example: polarized thinking breaks the entire issue down into only two sides—on one side, you're either for immigration or you're a racist. On the other side, it's either America first or amnesty for crooks and killers. In both cases, you either love America, or you don't. Note the naive simplification here: you're either for immigration or you're against it. All or nothing. No nuance, no complexity, no in-between. In reality, immigration reform involves a slew of important considerations, including human rights, taxes, unemployment, racism, unions, education, social services, multinational corporations, local governments, federalism, and abuse of illegal workers. The topic is not simple by any means, and polarized stances are an extremely naive approach to such a complex problem. Taking a dichotomous perspective may be easy, but it's an inadequate way to handle most large-scale social problems.

Sometimes it isn't so easy to identify the true concerns behind opposing perspectives. In the process of writing my previous book, *Disagreeing Agreeably*, I conducted thorough research on competing arguments surrounding some controversial political issues (such as affirmative action, gun control, immigration, and military spending). Admittedly, prior to writing the book, I was strongly on one side of each of those issues. After studying the strong counterarguments to my beliefs, however, I came to feel very differently about the issues, and about the people who held opposing opinions. My opinions on each of the issues softened, and in some cases changed. Even when my opinion didn't change, I came to understand where the other side was coming from, which immediately eliminated any hostility I felt toward those who disagreed with me. What this taught me was that simply understanding the perspectives of those who disagree with us alleviates anger, fear, and hostility.

Hatred and hostility are ultimately based on ignorance. When we truly understand other people's perspectives, it's very difficult to continue feeling hostility and hatred. As Henry Wadsworth Longfellow once said, "If we could read the secret history of our enemies, we should find in each man's life sorrow and suffering enough to disarm all hostility." It's easy to accept the explanation that those in the opposing party are just stupid and immoral, and it makes you feel happier and more self-satisfied in the short-term. Looking at things from the opposition's perspective takes more time and mental energy—and reduces your feelings of intellectual and moral superiority—but it also reduces anger, frustration, and hatred toward others.

Would you rather hold an ignorant view or an

enlightened one? Imagine what a better life you could lead if you replaced your anger and hatred with understanding and empathy.

How Dialectical Behavior Therapy Can Help

One effective technique we can use to combat dichotomous or polarized thinking is found in *Dialectical Behavior Therapy* (DBT). "As its name suggests, DBT is influenced by the philosophical perspective of dialectics: balancing opposites. [In clinical settings, a] therapist . . . works with the individual to find ways to hold two seemingly opposite perspectives at once, promoting balance and avoiding black and white—the all-or-nothing styles of thinking. In service of this balance, DBT promotes a *both-and* rather than an *either-or* outlook. The dialectic at the heart of DBT is acceptance and change."[74]

In other words, the practice of DBT helps people recognize and understand the inherent tradeoffs and gray areas that exist in the world.

When it comes to political issues specifically, there are almost always tradeoffs between opposing values and interests. Any law can be both good and bad at the same time, depending on your perspective. Any policy is likely to benefit one person while simultaneously harming another. It could also harm the same person in one way, while benefitting them in a different way. While polarized thinking focuses on only one benefit or harm, DBT seeks to identify other factors and consequences in order to provide a more complete and accurate picture of a policy's true implications. Again, a polarized approach is attractive because it's easier and makes us feel good about ourselves; the problem is that its seemingly apparent accuracy is false. It's an illusion that disregards the actual tradeoffs involved in any action. When I eat ice cream, it would be nice to focus only on the fact that it's delicious. But completely ignoring the risks of eating too much ice cream would have dangerous consequences for my cholesterol, appearance, energy, and even my relationships. Ignoring the inherent tradeoffs in political issues is just as wrongheaded as thinking only about the taste of ice cream while ignoring its health implications.

Again, people often have trouble coming up with the downsides to their preferred policies. Fortunately, there is an easy trick you can use. Recall that most political issues involve tradeoffs surrounding five fundamental values: Security, Opportunity, Freedom, Fairness, and Tranquility (SOFFT). In order to understand opposing perspectives on any policy-related question, you can go through each of the five values and consider how they might apply to the topic at hand. Even if you think a certain value isn't important to this issue, try to see how different values might still change someone's perspective on that issue. Remember that different people lead different lives, come from different cultures, hold different philosophical perspectives, and exist with different day-to-day circumstances, challenges, and needs. Just because a particular value's application to an issue seems irrelevant or inconsequential to *you* doesn't mean it's irrelevant to everyone else.

Treatment: Practice Dialectical Behavior Therapy

The purpose of this exercise is to identify those other value-based perspectives that surround a political question. Once you've identified the values that underlie opposing issue positions, you will likely realize that you also hold those values—you've just balanced their relevance in a different way. Note that recognizing opposing value-based concerns doesn't automatically mean that you're wrong and they're right. It is perfectly fine to hold an opinion of your own and to develop your own ideas about important political questions.

The purpose of DBT is not to determine who is right or wrong about an issue, but to understand the true basis for political disagreement. It provides a more complete picture of political challenges and the full implications of proposed solutions. Understanding that the other party is acting on values you share, and that they have reasonable arguments supporting their side, will make you more tolerant and willing to compromise in order to find the best way forward. It's not as self-gratifying as passively accepting the easy explanations you'll find in partisan circles, but it will give you a much more promising future.

Now it's your turn to practice DBT on your most important policies. For each of the policies you listed in Chapter 3, try your best to engage in dialectical thinking. Think of your preferred policy and then brainstorm how that policy would be good *and* bad. Which groups would that policy benefit? Which groups would it harm? Once you have identified the positives and negatives of your policies, you can use the templates below to create dialectical statements.

If the government [insert policy], it would result in [insert good thing], but it would also result in [insert bad thing].

This law would help [insert benefited group] while also harming [insert harmed group].

If you would like to explore DBT in greater depth, below are some useful links.

- <u>dbt.tools</u>: This website has a variety of excellent interactive tools for practicing DBT.
- <u>www.verywellmind.com/dialectical-behavior-therapy</u>: This page provides a general overview of DBT with short videos and additional resources.

CHAPTER 6

Living in Different Realities

*"The Party told you to reject the evidence of your eyes and
ears. It was their final, most essential command."*

—1984 by George Orwell

The human mind can believe anything when sufficiently
motivated. The Earth is flat! The moon landing was
a hoax. Lizard people control the world. The United
States government planned and executed the 9/11
terrorist attacks. Sandy Hook was a false flag. Leaders
of the Democratic Party are pedophiles. Vaccines cause
autism. The world is run by the Illuminati . . . or maybe
the Freemasons . . . no wait, they're the same people.
Aliens from the planet Nibiru will take over the world
on December 21, 2012. Ok, maybe that last one was
wrong. (Or is that what they want us to think?) These
are all beliefs that some seemingly intelligent and rational
people have held with extreme confidence. Yes, people are
capable of believing some pretty incredible things, even
when they make no sense.

In the early 1900s, psychiatrist Alfred Adler (a
founder of modern psychology) argued that individual
development arises out of the pursuit of objectives or
goals.[75] As the theory goes, an individual may have

suffered from some trauma in the past, but that trauma only affects their current state of mind to the extent that it alters their goals. For example, if someone is suffering from Generalized Anxiety Disorder (GAD), it may be because they want their environment to be more secure and predictable. An alcoholic might drink because they want more control in their life or to alleviate some internal pain. Some people get angry and yell when they feel overwhelmed and want to regain some control. The key to understanding a person's psychology, according to Adler, was to find the goal (desire) that underlies the problem behavior, then address that goal.

The human mind is a powerful tool that helps us in unseen ways to accomplish our goals. It makes us see the world the way we need to see it, and shows us a reality that suits our desires. If you want your favorite sports team to win, you're less likely to see fouls caused by your team, and more likely to see fouls committed by the other team. It's not that you're lying to yourself, it's just that your motivation can impact how you interpret events. The point is, if you want to understand why your mind does what it does, it's essential to first identify your mind's goals.

Partisanship plays into this by affecting our motivations. In her seminal article on motivated reasoning, psychologist Ziva Kunda explains that the way we "objectively" process new information actually depends on our desired outcome.[76] In simplified terms, we see only what we want to see, not necessarily the world as it really is—yet we remain confident that we're viewing our circumstances objectively and accurately. Motivated reasoning is our default way of processing information.

It's only when we're incentivized to pursue *accuracy* as our goal that we make more objective (though not perfect) judgments about our information and observations.

When your mind engages in motivated reasoning (which is almost all the time), it seeks out, interprets, and remembers information in a self-confirming manner, and it all happens beneath your conscious awareness. This means that when you're emotionally invested in your desired outcome, you can believe anything. In Adlerian psychology, the key to curing mental illness is to find the (usually unconscious) desire that motivates the problem behavior. Likewise, the key to curing partisanship is to identify precisely how it satisfies the beliefs you want to be true about yourself and about your world.

The purpose of this chapter is to explain how partisanship literally alters the way we experience reality. As we've already seen in previous chapters, partisanship motivates people to believe their party is superior to the other party. Under this assumption, irrational partisans are motivated to believe information that portrays their party as morally and intellectually superior to the opposition. Similar to addiction, partisanship creates an unconscious but powerful motivation that fundamentally distorts the way we're able to see and think. Unfortunately, we believe we are rational and unbiased, which prevents us from recognizing when we have a problem.

To paraphrase the film *A Beautiful Mind*, "Your mind is where the problem exists." Part of the solution lies in recognizing that our thinking is biased, and accepting that others might have legitimate reasons to disagree with our political opinions.

Fear and Insecurity

As the previous chapters explain, partisanship fosters fear and a sense of superiority. Because partisans tend to be isolated from members of the opposing party and their arguments, they inevitably come to distrust opposing partisans and view them as intellectually and morally inferior. Partisans accept this flattering picture of the world because it boosts their self-esteem. If the opposing party is evil, it's critical that they do not get power. After all, wars will break out, the world will end, you'll lose your job, and your children and pets will die! Both fear and the desire for a positive self-concept conspire to keep us looking at the world through our party's rose-colored glasses.

Perhaps this is the reason partisans so often engage in "whataboutisms" when leaders of their party act in obviously bad ways. As the flawed logic goes, "It doesn't matter that my party did X, because the other party did Y, which is so much worse than X." You see, it isn't about defending their own party; the primary motivation is to maintain superiority over the opposition. My party can never relinquish the relative moral high ground, no matter what happens. Doing so would acknowledge the possibility—no matter how infinitesimal—that the other party might be right, moral, intelligent, or righteous.

Maintaining relative superiority boosts partisans' self-esteem while giving them a reason to oppose the other party gaining any power. A partisan's primary motivation is *not* to hold accurate beliefs or to make the best decisions. Instead, partisans are incentivized to feel superior to others and to convince everyone else that the opposing party is an existential threat to humanity. Keeping these motivations in mind will help you better interpret the actions of partisans and understand how they can offer nonsensical arguments in support of their party. As we'll discover, partisans are so strongly motivated by pain avoidance and self-preservation that their minds will distort reality. That is why opposing partisans seem to live in completely different worlds.

Cognitive Dissonance

Let's take an even deeper look into how the human mind reacts to political disagreement. Cognitive dissonance takes place in all of our lives, and it's something we like to avoid.

It works like this: whenever we come across information that contradicts the reality we thought we knew, we experience a deep discomfort. For example, if I consider myself to be someone who is generally not foolish, and then I encounter evidence that I've been consistently making a choice that is foolish, the resulting feeling will be unpleasant, to say the least. In order to eliminate that discomfort, I'll be forced to do one of two things: either acknowledge that I have been behaving foolishly, which calls into question what I believe about myself, or reinterpret my behavior in a more favorable light, thus preserving my initial belief about myself. Until I've done one of those two things, the pain and discomfort will persist. Dissonance, then, becomes its own motivating factor. The desire to avoid cognitive dissonance subconsciously motivates us to avoid or favorably filter out information that contradicts our preferred opinions.

This behavior further reinforces the motivated reasoning from which it stems.

This is where another psychological phenomenon, known as "conditioned learning," comes into play. Any time you have a negative experience, your mind automatically makes associations between that experience and the immediate external stimuli. For example, if your hand gets too close to a flame and the fire burns you, your mind makes a strong association between the external stimulus (fire) and the negative outcomes (shock and pain). Consequently, your unconscious mind will seek to avoid future situations where fire might burn you. Our mind continues this learning process on an unconscious level, so we are rarely aware when it occurs. Few people remember the exact moment when they learned to avoid hot objects, but they know better than to place their hand on a stovetop burner.

Sometimes, these unconsciously derived associations are accurate—a fire will burn you. Other times, however, we incorrectly draw a connection between an external stimulus and an emotional experience. If you take a drug and then feel happier, your mind creates a learned association between the drug and happiness (this occurs even if the happiness is caused by situational factors unrelated to the drug). Let's say you only drink alcohol when you are out with friends, having a good time. Alcohol then becomes associated with happiness, even if it is actually the social interactions—not the alcohol— that cause the positive emotion. This is one reason why drug addiction is so pervasive and difficult to overcome.

Conversely, imagine getting an electric shock every time you watched a particular news channel. Wouldn't you eventually stop watching that channel to avoid the shock? That's exactly what happens when the partisan brain encounters dissonant information that challenges its beliefs about its own party; the brain pairs that information source with the feelings of anxiousness, nervousness, and distress generated by cognitive dissonance. Partisans respond by unconsciously seeking to avoid situations that might cause that negative mental state in the future. Consciously, they may rationalize their behavior using explanations that seem accurate to them even when those rationalizations are illogical. They believe they are simply doing the most rational thing.

Despite their best efforts to avoid it, partisans will inevitably encounter information that contradicts their preferred beliefs about reality. Not to fear: the mind has another trick hidden in its synapses. On the occasion when your party behaves truly shamefully, your partisan brain will still reward you for successfully defending your party.

Researchers conducted an interesting experiment just before the 2004 presidential election where they monitored the brain activity of partisans using an fMRI machine.[77] During the experiment, the researchers asked Democrats and Republicans to read inconsistent statements from their preferred candidate (John Kerry and George W. Bush, respectively). Upon reading the inconsistent statements, partisans at first felt anxiety (due to the painful cognitive dissonance that this discrepancy created). But then they did something interesting: they began to rationalize the inconsistent statements, determining that they were not really inconsistent after all. They then felt pleasure and relief. In other words, successfully defending their political party, though unmerited, made partisans feel happier and more self-satisfied. That's because our brains reward us for effectively engaging in motivated reasoning.

The more frequently your mind goes through this process of rationalization, the more conditioned it becomes to react through both avoidance and justification. Our motivations shape thousands of our tiny interpretations of the world, but our conscious mind only sees the end result: an apparent reality that obviously shows our desired beliefs are, in fact, correct. For irrational partisans, the end result of all those little misinterpretations is a completely warped sense of reality that can resemble extreme delusion. This is how partisanship becomes a mental illness, one rationalization at a time.

There is a digital mountain of research suggesting that our political beliefs are heavily driven by motivated reasoning. One prominent study asked participants to seek out and evaluate information regarding affirmative action and gun control.[78] Their results indicate that participants generally behave with a confirmation bias, meaning they seek out information from sources likely to confirm what they already believe.

For example, those in favor of gun control went to the National Rifle Association (NRA) to get their facts about gun legislation—ignoring the obvious bias of that information source. Additionally, the researchers found evidence for what's called biased interpretation, which occurs when we interpret reality in a way that supports what we want to believe. In the study, participants consistently rated arguments for their view as objectively strong, and those for opposing views as objectively weak. Finally, the researchers found participants engaging in selective memory, where they recalled information that supported their preferred opinion but conveniently forgot valid information that contradicted it. These three factors—confirmation bias, biased interpretation, and selective memory—each contribute to the power of motivated reasoning. Worst of all, this motivated reasoning process happens automatically and outside of conscious awareness. In other words, when we engage in motivated reasoning, we have no idea that it's happening.

Whether the mind engages in motivated reasoning and the extent to which it successfully defends the desired opinion depends largely on two factors. One factor is our ability to refute opposing information. Those with more political information about a topic are more likely to engage in motivated reasoning, simply because they have the information necessary to shoot down any opposing arguments. Ironically, those with less political information end up being less biased in their political opinions because they lack the information or arguments to successfully defend their position. This is why some very smart people adhere to some of the most delusional and idiotic beliefs. To defend some of the most bizarre conspiracy theories out there, believers must be informed enough to form counterarguments that refute any contradicting evidence that is thrown their way. The fact that the politically informed are more likely to engage in motivated reasoning is somewhat disheartening; it means that helping Americans become better informed about politics will not cure irrational partisanship.

Worst of all, this implies that the people with the most political power are least likely to see reality clearly, due to their partisan bias. Some of the most politically informed people are the elites who hold positions of power in government. A recent study looked at the reactions of politicians when they learned that their voters hold different opinions than they do about a public policy. It found that the political elites assume they know what's best—that they know more than their constituents, and therefore they are right.[79]

It may be true that the politician knows some information their constituents don't, but what's alarming is that they simply dismiss the thoughts and perspectives of their constituents by attributing their opinions to ignorance. Political elites assume they know the truth because they have more information. It can't be that they simply have different interests, or different perspectives on the world, or that the politician's perspective is biased in any way. Heck no! The most likely explanation is that voters simply are not smart enough to know what's good for them.

I hope you can see how motivated reasoning can lead politicians to these beliefs in the same way it misleads everybody else, convincing them that they are right and everybody else is wrong. And because they are well-versed in political rhetoric and information, political elites are better able to resist opposing arguments, and therefore more likely to remain entrenched in the distorted worldview that their unconscious motivations construct. In short, those who hold political power have more biased interpretations of reality than ordinary Americans.

Another important factor in motivated reasoning's success or failure is the strength of your motivation to hold a particular belief. For partisans, motivated reasoning runs the show to the extent they want their party to win and the other party to lose. The more a partisan dislikes or fears the opposing party, the more likely they are to inadvertently distort their own reality in ways that benefit their party. Partisans are personally incentivized to always regard their party in a positive light and to defend their party, no matter what. Defending their party, regardless of how terrible its actions might be sometimes, is necessary to maintain superiority and keep the other, evil party from gaining power. The more partisan a person is (meaning the more they fear the other party gaining power), the more likely they are to see the world in a distorted and incomplete way.

These unconscious motivations have important consequences for governmental effectiveness. For one, partisanship affects how people judge the actions of others, especially of politicians. Partisans interpret the motivations of government officials very differently depending on their political party. If a politician in our party does something we like, we attribute it to their strong moral character and intellectual superiority. In contrast, if a politician in the other party does the exact same thing, we attribute their behavior to political motivations or some other nefarious intent. Meanwhile, on the rare occasion that our guy does a bad thing, it's justified by the situation, or we assume it was just a one-time mistake. But if the other guy does the exact same bad thing, it's because he and his party are ignorant, immoral, and flat-out evil. These biased evaluations can lead us to support candidates who promote policies that negatively affect our lives.

In this way, partisanship undermines the accountability that's essential to a healthy democracy. When elected officials don't do what the public wants, the public must recognize that and vote them out of office. Partisanship prevents this accountability by creating an environment where elites tell voters what to think, and voters just believe them and rationalize away any evidence to the contrary. As a result, partisans are unlikely to hold their party's elites accountable. Worse, partisans will steadfastly vote against officials in the other party, even when they do things the public wants! We tell ourselves that they must have some ulterior motive. Perhaps they did the right thing, but it must have been for (what we perceive are) the wrong reasons, so we're going to vote against them—even though they did exactly what we wanted them to do. Our priority isn't accuracy or getting to the right outcome—it's expanding the power of our own party, even at the expense of our long-term wellbeing.

This is how partisanship prevents us from making quality voting decisions.

Like other mental illnesses, it can be hard to recognize you have a problem with partisanship, since your mind wants to believe that you're perfectly healthy and fine. One of the biggest problems in politics is our tendency to see our political beliefs as reflections of reality. We believe we see the world objectively, and that our political beliefs are simply the result of observing reality. This naive perspective makes it difficult for us to understand how someone else looking at the same reality could come to different conclusions about political affairs. There's a name for this in psychology: it's called *naive realism*. Under this perspective, it stands to reason that if other people look at the same reality, they should come to the exact same opinions that we do. And if our beliefs about the world differ from the beliefs of others, then one of us must be wrong. Further, the wrongness of our beliefs or theirs can only stem from a few possibilities: one of us lacks sufficient information or knowledge about the world; one of us is biased and non-objective in how we're interpreting that information; or, one of us might see the truth, but for self-interested reasons, choose to lie or otherwise act with intentional malice and selfishness.

Naive realism reduces the complexity of the world, convincing us that we know the full situation clearly and completely. It reduces the debate to a question of which of us is best informed and the most purely motivated. As you can see, partisans are likely to act as though their party is more intelligent, less biased, and more trustworthy than members of the other party. That is, our party sees the world as it really is, and the other party is ignorant at best, downright evil at worst.

Of course, there's a reason it's called *naive* realism. The naive part is that we believe there is only one correct set of conclusions to draw about reality, and that *we* are the ones capable of drawing those conclusions objectively.[80] Most of the time, when we have to come up with an explanation for why others disagree with us, by default we assume the problem is with them. The reason for this stems from the *bias blind spot*.[81] In brief, the bias blind spot occurs when human beings notice bias in other people's opinions, but not in their own.

Yet another psychological phenomenon that exacerbates this problem is the *introspection illusion*.[82] From time to time, we suspect that our opinions may be biased. As reasonable human beings, we then evaluate our own biases, assuming that our self-evaluation methods are objective. Surprise! We rarely find significant evidence of bias. As a result, we conclude that our opinions objectively reflect reality. Our ability to find biases in our own views is limited by our unconscious motivation to not see that bias. We don't find bias because we don't want to.

Bringing this back to politics, since partisans conclude that they are not biased by their partisanship but instead see the world as it really is, they respond to events in a way that benefits their party without ever recognizing the distortion that's happening. Partisans end up becoming even more confident after engaging in this process of falsely reassuring introspection. They think they have evaluated their own biases, found none, and are now doubly sure that their opinions are reflections of objective reality. By extension, their assumption that the other party must be wrong becomes reinforced. If my beliefs are objective reflections of reality, as confirmed by introspection (though a phony process), then the other party must be wrong. Their input is simply inferior, and it must be because they are either ignorant or immoral.

Combine all these mental processes with the emotional allure of partisan identity and it becomes clear how people can believe absolutely ridiculous and downright dangerous things. Our unconscious mind will convince us that 2+2=5 if it is necessary for our party to win the election. Imagine that all the political leaders in your party, your preferred partisan media sources, and all your friends and family told you that 2+2 actually does equal 5, and that the other party had brainwashed you into thinking 2+2=4. In such a scenario, do you really think you would continue holding the correct opinion? More likely, you would come to assume that the leaders of your political party know something you don't know. Despite everything you've been taught about basic math, you would most likely trust your party and conform to the belief that 2+2=5, especially if it seemed to be the only way your party could win the election and keep the other party out of power.

This is the result of irrational partisanship—actions based on shared group motives, rather than logic or fact. At that point, you no longer belong to a political party. You're in a cult!

Similarities to Addiction

When we put all of this together, we discover that the mental state of a partisan is quite similar to that of an addict. This comparison may seem extreme, but the mental processes are fundamentally very similar.

At the root of alcoholism, before the chemicals take over, is some deep desire that pushes the person to drink. As a result, they interpret events in a way that justifies drinking. "I need to celebrate." "I had a bad day at work." "It's just one beer, I can control it this time." Even though those explanations are clearly selective, incomplete, and contrary to their previous experiences, the alcoholic remains blind to any disconfirming evidence. These arguments are good enough for them, even in the face of conflicting information, because they support what the alcoholic wants—another drink.

The alcoholic is motivated to believe that they did, indeed, have a bad day, because that belief justifies drinking, and so they'll see only those events of the day that confirm the desired outcome. And then what happens when they drink? Their brain rewards them even before the alcohol has had any chemical effect. They feel better the moment they take that first sip. Alcohol takes at least a few minutes to be absorbed into the bloodstream and reach the brain, and it isn't possible for the drug to cause an effect that immediate. The pleasure the alcoholic instantly feels is their brain rewarding them for drinking (achieving the goal of their unconscious motivations). If you were to convince an alcoholic that a beverage contained alcohol when it didn't, they would feel the same pleasure after that initial sip. They wouldn't feel that anything is lacking until eventually realizing there was no alcohol. Alcoholics are so motivated to get the associated effects of alcohol that their minds interpret reality in a way that justifies their desire to drink.

Perhaps you are thinking that alcoholism is different because it's a drug and there is no external partisan chemical that gets ingested and sent to the brain. But ingested chemicals are not required to create an addiction—people become addicted to eating, gambling, and sex, even though none of those behaviors involve injecting or consuming any toxic or addictive drugs. Yet in each of these examples, the pattern is the same: the person is motivated toward a particular desire, which causes them to filter and interpret incoming information in a biased way to satisfy that motivation. This occurs regardless of whether it's fed by alcohol, gambling, food, sex, or even political victory.

Similar to partisanship, addictive behavior sneaks up gradually and is caused by a mix of physiology and life experiences. On a positive note, the parallel between addiction and partisanship extends to recovery. From addiction recovery, we can learn how to walk away from partisanship's grasp.

Our motivations alter the way we handle information. For partisans, the main motive is not necessarily to be accurate, but to be *right*. This—when fueled by the trifecta of confirmation bias, interpretation bias, and selective memory—makes us behave in unconsciously motivated ways that can become extremely irrational. It makes us ridiculously and increasingly self-contradictory, harming even our own self-interest. Meanwhile, more political education is not unhelpful, but it actually makes us even more entrenched in our views.

The effects of these unconscious motivations matter—our country's economic state, social currency (trust level), political accountability, and wellbeing all suffer when we succumb to the sway of irrational partisanship. Like an alcoholic, when we wear partisan goggles, we can't see how we've distorted our own interpretations of the world. After a while, the only thing that matters is that we feel like we're in the right group, on the right side of history. Our brains will bend to make reality meet that desire.

Thankfully, there is a solution: by eliminating our partisan motives and replacing them with a desire for accuracy, we can recover from this sickness.

How do you stop partisanship from distorting your reality? To answer that question, let's look at how alcoholics successfully stop drinking, gamblers stop gambling, and smokers stop smoking. The best and most effective way to stop addictive behavior is to take away the addict's motivation to engage in the addictive behavior. Gambling addictions are the most similar to irrational partisanship since there is no external chemical being administered, so let's look at this one further.

The addicted mind of the gambler focuses on very

particular pieces of reality in order to justify their continued gambling. The best way for them to bring an end to the gambling habit is to bring their life's priorities into focus. As they turn their focus to their broader life goals and desires, gambling's net negative effect on those goals starts to come into view. Focusing on their personal life objectives shifts their desires away from gambling and toward more fulfilling endeavors. Addiction is complex and varies from individual to individual, but refocusing their motivation is a critical component of any addict's recovery.

This provides a lesson on how we can address the pathologies of partisanship. It's critical that we weaken the underlying motivation for party adherence and replace it with the larger goal of accuracy. If you take away the desire that drives unhealthy drinking behavior and replace it with new desires, the mind will no longer alter its perceptions around the motivation to drink. Likewise, if you take away the fear of the other party and restructure your goals to prioritize accuracy, your mind will no longer be at the mercy of unconscious motivations that warp your view of reality.

How do we eliminate partisan motivation? It's a difficult task, to put it mildly. Unfortunately, there is no singular way to eliminate our human tendency to engage in motivated reasoning, but we can retune our motivations. We can address the root of those processes that, below our consciousness, would destroy us. That is precisely what Part 3 of this book is about. Each chapter in Part 3 will provide specific strategies to reduce the underlying motivation to see one party win and the other party lose. Altogether, these approaches can help bring us away from partisanship and back to reality.

Treatment: Understand Your Motivations

Before we move on, it's important to understand the extent of our partisan motivations. Again, because these motivations are unconscious, we are rarely aware that we have them. So, how do we measure unconscious motivations? Well, it's certainly not an exact science, but there are a few questions that provide a rough measure of partisan motivated reasoning.

In particular, the goal here is to measure how much you are motivated to see one party in power—or the other party out of power. The more you identify with a political party, hope to see them win the next election, or conversely fear another party gaining political power, the more susceptible you are to partisan motivated reasoning. To be clear, just because you prefer one party over another does not mean you have a mental illness, but the strength of your desires helps assess your level of risk.

Below is a series of questions that measure your internal motivation to see your party win the election. Once again, it is important that you are honest with yourself and answer the questions as truthfully as possible. No one will see your answers, so you have no reason to feel ashamed. To quote Dave Chappelle: "If there's hate in your heart, let it out!"

For each of the following statements, record whether you personally believe the statement is true or false. At the end, tally up all your "true" responses. The more times you answer "true" to the questions below, the more susceptible you are to partisan motivated reasoning and the overall ill effects of irrational partisanship.

- True or False: If the other party gets into power, America will never recover.
- True or False: I'm frequently afraid of what will happen if the other party wins the presidency.
- True or False: Worrying about a presidential election has caused me to lose sleep.
- True or False: Sometimes I wish bad things would happen to people in the other Party.
- True or False: I have hoped that a president in the other party would die while they were in office.
- True or False: When someone criticizes my political party, it feels like they're attacking me.
- True or False: My party identity is a big part of who I am.
- True or False: I can't think of any area where I agree with the other party.
- True or False: There is no point in talking with the other party.
- True or False: If the other party controls the federal government, they will ruin my life.
- True or False: Thinking about the other party makes me afraid.
- True or False: Thinking about the other party makes me angry.
- True or False: I don't have any friends in the other party.

CHAPTER 7

How Intellectual Humility Can Cure Partisanship

"I am better off than he is—for he knows nothing and thinks that he knows. I neither know nor think that I know. In this latter particular, then, I seem to have slightly the advantage of him."

—Socrates

In the quote above, Socrates explains how it could be that he is wiser than others, yet admittedly doesn't know much of anything. This isn't false humility. After speaking with supposedly wise and advanced men—the ones with titles, education, and authority—Socrates realized they didn't have much insight, yet they were overly confident in their own thoughts and in what knowledge they did possess. Socrates concluded that real wisdom requires that we recognize the limits of our understanding. In other words, wisdom is not what you know about a topic; rather, wisdom stems from your awareness that there's stuff you *don't know* about the topic.

What we can learn from Socrates is this: it matters how we perceive our own knowledge. If we find ourselves feeling absolute correctness in our opinions, that we *know* the answer, it's actually a personal weakness, a character flaw, and likely to let us down. In this sense, confidence in one's own opinions and beliefs is actually a weakness and not a strength.

Thousands of years ago, Socrates recognized the power of *intellectual humility*, or the personal awareness that our beliefs and perceptions may be wrong. Intellectual humility is the recognition that I might not have all of the relevant information, that my thinking and logic could be fallible, and ultimately that my beliefs might be incorrect.[83]

Intellectual humility requires two things. First is an understanding and awareness that the information you have access to may be biased or incomplete. Second is a general acceptance that your views may simply be wrong in any situation.

Although the concept of intellectual humility is nothing new, scholars have just recently begun to examine its benefits.[84] Research suggests that practicing intellectual humility makes us more intellectually curious, open-minded, and overall better listeners.[85] Intellectual humility also appears to increase: empathy, altruism, benevolence, respect for humanity, support for mutually beneficial negotiation, and tolerance of opposing viewpoints.[86] Most importantly in our discussion of partisanship, intellectual humility makes us less defensive about our beliefs, which means we gather information in a less biased manner. Specifically, the higher we score in intellectual humility, the more likely we are to seek out balanced arguments on political topics, and to objectively evaluate the strength of political arguments.[87] In other words, intellectual humility retunes our objectives, leading us away from the self-satisfying behaviors of motivated reasoning and toward more objectively beneficial solutions.[88]

In this chapter, we'll explore intellectual humility

as a method for treating our own irrational beliefs and perspectives. If practicing intellectual humility improves our rationality, objectivity, levels of civility, and collaboration, then what are some ways we can use it to combat widespread irrational partisanship and motivated reasoning?

First, we'll explore why intellectual humility is the most logical and appropriate stance to take in any situation, given our limited knowledge and propensity for mental biases (see Chapter 6). Second, we'll look at the surprising discovery that being more humble in your beliefs actually makes you a more intelligent, likable, and happier person. Third, we'll learn how practicing more intellectual humility can reduce hostility between opposing partisans (and between you and your family and friends too). Finally, I'll provide specific strategies you can use to raise the level of humility in yourself and, amazingly, people you're talking to.

Why Humility Is a Superpower

Why bother learning to be more humble? Why should we practice intellectual humility, especially when we're engaging with people who are spouting ridiculous conspiracy theories they saw on Facebook? Don't they need to be corrected? Isn't it better to stay firm than cede to their illogical arguments?

Put simply, we should be humble because we don't know everything. The world is complex. To think that only you know how to fix what ails society—or how to fix any of its problems—is, to put it mildly, foolish. The world is immensely complicated, and yet so many people believe they know what the world needs in order to function well. Intellectual humility acknowledges the absurdity of this belief, which is the first step in reaching a real solution to any given problem.

Since we don't know everything there is to know about political issues, it's better to be humble than arrogant in our beliefs. There could always be information we're not familiar with, or even aware of. To claim otherwise is foolish and closed-minded. Consider any one of your political opinions. Can you guarantee there's nothing you could possibly learn in the future that might change your perspective? It's impossible to answer that question with a confident 'yes,' because you don't know what evidence you're currently unaware of. If we can acknowledge that we don't have incomplete information about the world, that is sufficient reason to remain intellectually humble when it comes to our current thoughts and beliefs. No matter how much we know, we can always learn more. And the set of all the things we don't know will always be far larger than the set of all the things we do know.

Not only are there far more things we don't know than things we do know, but many of the things we think we know are also inaccurate. Remember from Chapter 6 that motivated reasoning influences us on an unconscious level, so there are likely biases or distortions in our interpretations that we're not aware of. We could be wrong even while vehemently declaring that we're right. How fervently we believe something to be true is not a litmus test for how true that belief is, so don't be fooled by your own confidence or the confidence of others when it comes to political opinions.

The political information you hold is likely incomplete

and may be biased by numerous other factors, including self-interest, ideology, partisan blind spots, or information sources. Since it is impossible to know with certainty that your perspective is entirely unpolluted, intellectual humility is the correct stance to take. In other words, these two criteria—the possibility that there's something you don't know, and the possibility that what you do know could be incorrect—indicate that intellectual humility, not intellectual arrogance, is the best stance.

It is important to point out that not all beliefs should be held with humility. Indisputable facts about the world, previous events, and definitional truths can (usually) be held with arrogance. For example, you can hold the knowledge that 2+2=4 with intellectual arrogance, just like I know that the earth is round and revolves around the sun. Although we certainly should not hold every belief with humility, we too often err in the other direction and hold beliefs with arrogance, even when we lack sufficient knowledge to support that stance. In short, accepting that your political opinions might be at least slightly wrong is the most logical and rational attitude for approaching political problems, given your mental biases and the incompleteness of your information. In contrast, the intellectually arrogant stance is "I know how this works and there is no way I am wrong." Does that ever sound like you?

How Humility Improves Your Wellbeing

Finding more opportunities to exercise humility can benefit your general wellbeing in a number of ways. Most importantly, intellectual humility improves your ability to learn and make better decisions. Research shows that intellectual humility is strongly related to two of the Big 5 personality traits: Agreeableness and Openness to new ideas.[89]

If you possess the trait of 'Openness,' that means you're more intellectually curious and less likely to engage in polarized thinking.[90] In other words, intellectually humble people find more joy in thinking, and devote more effort to evaluating new information. Additionally, if you accept that your beliefs might be wrong, you're less likely to suffer from cognitive dissonance when you encounter conflicting information. Recall from the last chapter that cognitive dissonance is that feeling of mental discomfort you get when you encounter information that contradicts your beliefs.[91] When you take an intellectually arrogant stance, you'll feel immense internal pressure to avoid and argue away anything that conflicts with your current beliefs.

One study found that those who scored lower in intellectual humility experienced intensely negative reactions while reading arguments they didn't like, and very positive reactions while reading arguments that supported their political views.[92] If the intellectually arrogant find it mentally taxing to alleviate cognitive dissonance, they're more likely to both consciously and subconsciously avoid opposition in the first place—which leads to even more bias and distortion in their thinking over time.

In contrast, the more you embrace intellectual humility, the less aversion you feel toward hearing out any argument or opinion.[93] Since the intellectually humble run into less cognitive dissonance, they are mentally and emotionally unburdened, and therefore free (and more likely) to actively seek out information from sources that present alternative perspectives.[94] In other words, people with more intellectual humility feel better in the face of conflicting information or opinions, and because they feel better, they are more likely to explore different sources of information and thus make better decisions.

Spending more time with those who hold political opinions that are different from yours can help you understand their perspectives more completely. Although exposure to opposing arguments is a necessary first step, it may not immediately work to reduce political hostility. That's because when you are motivated to defend your position, you tend to rate arguments that support your pre-existing opinions as strong and of high quality, and instead rate opposing arguments as weak or unfounded.[95]

Interestingly, even the *exact same* argument will be judged as stronger when it comes from a like-minded source.[96] This means that when you feel defensive about your opinion, exposure to opposing arguments can potentially make you feel more confident in your opinion, without any new rational merit to hold it up.[97] If partisans are convinced that the opposition's perspectives are backed only by bad logic and bad information, it shouldn't be surprising when they conclude that those who disagree with them are ignorant or biased.[98]

Reducing political hostility requires us to study opposing arguments and objectively evaluate their quality. Intellectual humility provides a path for anyone to do these two things, which makes us more likely to seek out balanced arguments and objectively evaluate them.[99] Not only are the intellectually humble more likely to seek out opposing arguments, but they are more likely to acknowledge their legitimacies. When we're not aware of the validities in opposing perspectives, we tend to attribute those opinions to negative and unflattering causes.[100] In fact, partisans "under the influence" of irrationality are more likely to attribute positive, "pure" motivations to members of their party, and negative, tainted motivations to members of the opposing party.[101] But if we maintain our intellectual humility, we will recognize that opposing perspectives can also be rational, which makes us less likely to assume bias or ignorance, and also less likely to harbor negative feelings.[102]

Perhaps the most compelling benefit that intellectual humility offers to counteract hostility is that it makes no sense to hate someone who may turn out to be right. If you accept that you might possibly be wrong and that the other person might be right, it's self-defeating to hate them simply because they hold a different opinion. Politically, those who exercise intellectual humility are less likely to divide issues into camps of right and wrong. Instead, they'll recognize that a situation may not have one correct, fully satisfying solution, and that some political problems will (and should) involve an ever-present tension and non-resolution. As Leary and colleagues explain, "intellectually humble people . . . recognize that few issues are black-and-white and that reasonable arguments can be made on both sides of many debates." In other words, they engage in dialectical, rather than polarized, thinking about political issues.

Studies suggest that intellectually humble people live with a higher tolerance for this kind of ambiguity, meaning that they are more comfortable with the fact that many political problems and questions do not have conclusive answers.[103] And if there is no conclusive singular correct answer to a political problem, like how much the government should spend on education each year, then it may well be that both my position and your position on that issue are equally valid.

Studies also show that intellectual humility lowers feelings of animosity between people in the midst of disagreement. For example, Leary and colleagues asked participants to read essays on topics of religion and then asked them how they felt about the authors. Those who scored higher in intellectual humility gave more positive evaluations of all the essay writers, regardless of whether they agreed with the points made in the essays. In contrast, "participants low in intellectual humility consistently derogated writers who expressed antireligious sentiments relative to writers of pro-religion and balanced essays."[104] Likewise, one study found that intellectual humility correlated with increased tolerance among religious leaders.[105]

Another experiment raised intellectual humility in some participants by explaining the benefits of a growth mindset of intelligence, which says intelligence can be cultivated and is not a fixed attribute. Adopting a growth mindset makes us more accepting of the fact that we might be wrong in our views, because we see being wrong as an essential part of the learning process. When we become more intellectually humble in our views, we also become less hostile toward those who hold opposing political beliefs.[106] In other words, intellectually humble people are less likely to judge others based on predetermined characteristics, and more likely to hear out arguments based on their own merit.

The more we believe specific issue disagreements are generally based on reasonable differences of opinion, the less likely we are to view politics as a struggle of us vs. them, liberals vs. conservatives, or Republicans vs. Democrats. Practicing intellectual humility can turn your conversations in the direction of openness, collaborative problem-solving, and real dialogue, rather than leading to outrage and defensiveness.

Intellectual humility helps open your eyes to the fact that other people hold legitimate reasons for their opinions. Not only will you end up feeling better about them, but you'll be in a far better state to actually have a productive conversation where you can learn something new (and they can too). Raising your own level of intellectual humility helps keep conversations on an objective foundation, and as a result, softens hostility while improving your communication and problem-solving skills. In short, practicing intellectual humility makes you more rational.

Intellectual humility can also help you evaluate your own party's positioning. It's important to remain intellectually humble when it comes to evaluating your party's official issue positions so that you don't arrogantly assume your party is right and has it all figured out. We often feel more confident in the correctness of our beliefs when other people hold the same views as we do— and especially when there's an official logo behind that position. Unfortunately, in this case, strength in numbers can make us overconfident. Party validation strengthens our certainty and confidence—but it's unmerited and does nothing to advance our understanding. The certainty of the group and the officialness of the party's stamp of approval might make you think, "Hey, it's not just me who believes this is right . . . all my friends, family, and my entire party agree with me! How can we all be wrong?" This may seem reasonable enough until you realize everyone in your party shares in the same propensities for self-confirming and self-satisfying validation-seeking that you have, which can cause the exact same false reassurance in the larger group's agreement.

What's more, those who have allowed partisanship to become too important in their lives want their party to win the next election, and are therefore motivated to accept whatever explanations put their party in a better light than the opposition. If so many in your group are similarly motivated, then it's not surprising if those affiliated with the group are simultaneously wrong about the same thing. This is a phenomenon known as "groupthink," which occurs when you find more confidence in your beliefs by talking in a group of others who already agree with you.

In these "groupthink" scenarios, you gain more confidence because you believe that you can't all be wrong. But you can! It has been "commonly known" that the earth is flat, that leeches and bloodletting can heal you of illness, and that we are the center of the solar system. This is why we must apply intellectual humility to our party's opinions and stances. Partisans must constantly accept that their party might be wrong in both big and small ways. This is especially true when a policy outcome will benefit the party's electoral fortunes. You must accept the fact that you could be wrong, even when most or even all of your fellow partisans agree with you.

How to Increase Intellectual Humility

There are many ways to build a habit of true intellectual humility in yourself, as well as bring it out in others. One simple way to do this is to pay attention to how you speak. The small words you choose have a big impact on the way you think and behave, and subtle changes in your words can cause you to see the world with more intellectual humility. In the same way that using more positive and optimistic words makes you actually feel more positive and optimistic, using intellectually humble words can make you more humble in your beliefs.

What are these magic linguistic weapons? Choosing to say "I believe" or "I think" instead of "I know" is one. This small choice helps to remind you that you might be wrong. It also makes it OK if you are wrong because you haven't committed to knowing. It can also be helpful to use the word "usually" instead of "always," and "most likely" or "may be" rather than "definitely" or "will be." Shift attention to your arguments instead of yourself by prefacing statements with "some people would argue" instead of "I would argue" or "I think." This can help your audience focus more on your ideas.

Using more humble words in place of overconfident ones will change the way you perceive situations and leave you open to different perspectives, but it also makes others a lot more receptive to your perspective. Rather than talking about things as absolute certainties, introducing your thoughts with words like "it seems to me" or "in my experience" shows others that you're not trying to claim all-knowingness, which makes them more likely to listen to you. Over time, using humble language will provide constant self-reminders that you are not absolutely sure about your grasp on complex situations (such as political issues) that are extremely deep and clouded with uncertainty.

Although learning to be more humble in your beliefs is the ultimate goal, realize that it will take some time and practice to make using humble words a habit. There's an even faster tool you can use to be more humble: force yourself to explain *causality* (i.e. "X causes Y, and Y causes Z, which then impacts Q...")。Don't leave any part blank, and where there are gaps in your knowledge, acknowledge them. Previous research refers to this as a "mechanistic explanation," which is a fancy term for trying to explain fully how something works.[107]

In a fascinating experiment, researchers asked participants to provide a thorough explanation detailing the causal links involved in a political policy. By requiring participants to elaborate on the causal process and then judging the thoroughness of that explanation, the study made participants more aware of just how complex the issue was, and how much they did not actually understand about the topic. In other words, it made people more humble by undermining their self-assuredness and revealing the gaps in what they thought they knew. Importantly, the researchers further found that asking for a mechanistic explanation led participants to hold less extreme opinions and made them more amicable toward people with different perspectives.

The next time you're having trouble understanding how anyone could be so stupid as to disagree with you, try creating an elaborate causal explanation for how your preferred policy will affect society. Then consider how confident you are about each step in your causal process. Keep in mind that it is extremely difficult to prove causation, especially when it comes to social and economic phenomena, which are inherently complex. When you start to think in this way, you'll begin to understand just how complex societal issues really are.

Pushing yourself through a mechanistic explanation can help you develop a more humble attitude and awareness of your limitations. You can also use this as a tool to encourage humility in others. If you are discussing politics with a partisan, try simply asking, "how would that work?" The more you inquire about the specific causal processes involved in a policy, the more humble the partisan is likely to become, for multiple reasons. First, when they're asked to give a mechanistic explanation, they'll become more aware of the gaps in their understanding, and they'll realize their information is incomplete. Second, your question expresses curiosity rather than attack. When we feel attacked (for example, when we're told we're wrong, arrogant, or unaware of ourselves), we're more likely to become defensive. In contrast, curiosity that makes us think more thoroughly lets us arrive at our own conclusions, and it does so in a context that's open and receptive, rather than threatening.

Once you develop more humility in your own perspective and approach, then you can take steps to foster humility in others. This is how societal trends shift: one conversation at a time. Each time you introduce or encourage an attitude of intellectual humility, you're creating another ripple in society at large. The humility you model in your interactions can be infectious—you just might change someone's life by seeing things through their perspective, and by helping them to see things from a different perspective as well.

The simplest way to do this is to just be humble yourself! Serve as a role model of intellectual humility to others by admitting when you don't know something, or when you are uncertain or have doubts. When people see you being humble rather than arrogant in your beliefs, they're more likely to let their guard down and behave with more humility and curiosity as well. Furthermore, when you demonstrate humble openness in a political discussion, others are likely to feel an instinctive need to reciprocate that humility.

Try it the next time you have a discussion with someone. Just admit when you don't know something, acknowledge that you might be wrong, or that you probably don't have all of the relevant information on the topic. Most of the time, others will respond with more humility as well. Of course, this strategy won't work 100 percent of the time. Some people will remain know-it-alls for the rest of their insecure, ignorant, and isolated lives. But most will open up, soften up, and step into a level of intellectual humility that mirrors yours. And remember that intellectual arrogance is contagious as well—the more certainty and arrogance you bring to conversations, the more defensive reactions you'll get.

You might feel afraid to express uncertainty or weakness in an argument. Maybe you think others might think you're dumb if you hesitate or communicate that you're not certain. But I can tell you that people do not think you are dumb when you are humble, honest, and candid about what you know. They may think you're dumb for other reasons, but it won't be because of your humility.

However, I can pretty much guarantee that if you refuse to listen to other opinions while simultaneously communicating that your opinions are clearly correct, you'll ruin a lot of relationships and be lonelier as a result. Responding to others with statements like, "I've never thought of that," or "that's a good point that I hadn't considered" expresses open-mindedness and a desire to find the best solution. When you openly admit that you don't know everything, it makes others more comfortable talking to you and softens their defensive posture. When you do so, you are indicating that it's OK to be wrong and to not have the whole thing figured out. Once you have admitted that you are fallible, others will feel more comfortable admitting that they could be wrong or that they may be missing some of the pieces as well. Instead of deafly defending their beliefs, they'll seek out more information in the search for a better answer. In short, the most useful thing you can do to increase intellectual humility in others and facilitate productive discussions is to communicate your own humility through the words you use, how you listen, and your willingness to admit what you don't know.

The two institutions best equipped to foster intellectual humility on a large scale are schools and the media. Both of these institutions influence the ideas we consider and accept, and the attitude with which we process those ideas. These institutions have an opportunity to foster intellectual humility by focusing more attention on the unknowns, ambiguities, and uncertainties surrounding complex issues. Rather than sharing information as though it's fully known, these institutions could instead facilitate real conversations around questions that remain unanswered.

Educational institutions in particular should focus on what we don't know, at least as much as what we do know. There's an inclination among educators to focus on the many things that have been discovered or that can be cleanly and succinctly discussed, while shying away from topics or questions that are open-ended or have only ambiguous answers. But this approach promotes intellectual arrogance because it tells students that uncertainty is unacceptable. In reality, it is perfectly acceptable and often important to respond to a question with "I don't know" or "I'm not sure."

Another awareness-boosting approach that educators can try is requiring students to submit detailed causal explanations about a particular political topic (such as immigration reform or gun control), then have them conduct an in-depth analysis of competing perspectives around the issue. Then have students look back on their initial understanding of the issue and identify gaps where they lacked knowledge at the time of the initial assignment (and consider all the unknown gaps they may still have). Importantly, throughout this process, educators should ask students to consider the uncertainties that surround the issue. This exercise shatters the illusion of complete understanding and breeds humility instead of arrogance.

The news media is another institution with an opportunity to promote intellectual humility, especially in the way they frame political controversies. In their analysis of a political situation, media broadcasters could focus on the lack of information at hand, the challenges that experts are still debating, and the uncertainties that surround the consequences of public policies. It would also go a long way if, instead of framing debates in terms of generic worldview, those in the media shared the actual arguments at play.

Journalists commonly present policy debates as "Democrats argue X while Republicans argue Y." One of the problems with this extraordinarily simplified statement is that partisans often hear it and immediately attribute the other party's resistance to ignorance, bias, and general stubborn-headedness. It also feeds right into the self-validating motivation to believe whatever is most flattering for one's political party. Instead, it might be more productive to say something like, "some argue X or Y, while others argue Z" or "it is possible that X, but Y could also be true." This acknowledgement of uncertainty can help others to accept their own cognitive limitations. These small changes in the way journalists present political issues could go a long way in creating a social environment in the US that is more humble and less blindly partisan.

Socrates recognized something that many people miss: it's better to pay attention to how much you don't know, than to pretend that what you don't know doesn't matter. When we oversimplify and overreach, our arrogance begins to show. The simple (though not always easy) countermeasure is to constantly remind yourself to practice intellectual humility. When you feel yourself becoming frustrated over an issue that seems like it shouldn't still be a problem, or if a conversation is going in circles, try to remind yourself that the world is much bigger and more complicated than you or any single human being can comprehend. Try to bring genuine curiosity to those with different opinions by asking questions like "how might that work?"

CHAPTER 7 | HOW INTELLECTUAL HUMILITY CAN CURE PARTISANSHIP **119**

As you make the small changes discussed in this chapter, you'll find yourself becoming happier, more likable, clearer-headed, and an all-around better person.

Treatment: Practice Intellectual Humility

Before moving on to the next chapter, let's practice intellectual humility with your most important issues and policies. Once you understand how to make yourself more humble on these topics, you can practice humility in all sorts of political and nonpolitical situations. After all, intellectual humility is useful and beneficial in all of your interactions, not just those concerning politics.

To practice humility, let's return to your list of most important issues and policies from Chapter 3. For each of the issues, write down what information would help you have a better understanding of the topic. What research would you like to see concerning these issues? Try to think of the things you *don't* know about the issues, but would like to know. In what ways is your information limited? Do the same for your preferred policies.

Additionally, ask yourself "What would it take to change my mind about this policy?" Another way to phrase this is, "If my preferred policy resulted in [insert bad outcome], I would oppose it." If your answers to these questions are "nothing," then you do not have an opinion, you have an assumption. And we all know what assumptions make you.

Additional Resources

If you're interested in this topic, here are some useful resources that provide a more extensive understanding of intellectual humility and some tools to practice it more thoroughly:

www.templeton.org/discoveries/intellectual-humility
characterlab.org/playbooks/intellectual-humility/

wisdomcenter.uchicago.edu/news/wisdom-news/what-does-intellectual-humility-look

CHAPTER 8

A Rational Cure for Irrational Partisanship

"If the Martians ever find out how human beings think, they'll kill themselves laughing."

–Albert Ellis

I hate going to the doctor. Can you blame me? First, you sit in a waiting room for an indefinite period of time, surrounded by complete strangers who are sick, in pain, and mostly miserable. Relief from this awkward situation happily comes when an overworked, underpaid, and unsurprisingly disgruntled nurse calls your name. The nurse proceeds to check your vitals, which amounts to a glaring reminder that you're shorter, fatter, and have higher blood pressure than you'd like. Then, just in case you needed more time to ruminate on your physical inadequacies, they put you in a room to wait in absolute silence for an excruciatingly long time. Finally, a doctor stops by to poke you, prod you, and probably perform some degrading medical procedure before informing you of the regimen of drugs you'll be taking for at least the next few months. And don't even get me started on dentists, as I'm pretty sure all of their instruments were designed by sadists.

Is it any wonder people avoid consulting with medical professionals until after their problem has become intolerable? Fortunately, getting help from a mental health professional is far less painful than visiting a doctor or dentist. Given modern technology, mental health care can even be provided in virtual settings from the comfort of your home, allowing you to skip the awkward waiting room scene entirely. Even better, you can practice many of the most powerful (non-prescription) mental health treatments on your own, sometimes without the need of professional support at all.

Of all the available forms of mental health therapy, Rational Emotive Behavior Therapy (REBT) is uniquely qualified to address irrational partisanship. One of the most influential voices in the development of modern psychology, Dr. Albert Ellis formulated REBT based on the simple idea that most of our emotional and behavioral problems result from unrealistic beliefs and expectations. As I explained in previous chapters, irrational partisanship (i.e., over-prioritizing party identity in your life) stems from inaccurate perceptions of the people associated with the opposing party and a consuming desire to feel superior to them. REBT directly attacks the roots that lead to each of these distortions.

First, REBT deploys something called the ABC model (which we'll discuss later in this chapter) to help us identify our irrational beliefs, question the foundation of those beliefs, and then replace them with new, more mature, well-formed, and dependable ones. Second, REBT advocates "unconditional self-acceptance" (USA) to undermine the personal insecurities that drive partisans to knock others down so they can feel superior. Importantly, USA can also help you develop a real comfort with being proven wrong and with the possibility that your party might be wrong in specific circumstances. Third, REBT employs a particularly useful tool for curing partisanship, called "unconditional other acceptance" (UOA), which can help you deal with the irrational partisans you meet in life. UOA supports productive ongoing interactions with others, even when they fail to meet your expectations for how they ought to think and behave. Finally, REBT can reduce your fear of undesired political events by helping you distinguish between what you need and what you want. Altogether, the tools of REBT can be a powerful self-improvement approach to dealing with the psychological causes of irrational partisanship.

From a more practical standpoint, REBT has some important advantages over other psychological tools. For one, REBT is fundamentally a shift in perspective, and as such does not require specific guidance from a therapist. Instead, anyone can use the techniques of REBT to improve their life privately and on their own time. Additionally, unlike some other self-improvement techniques, REBT does not rely on mystical thinking or pseudoscience. Instead, it asks you to use rational reflection and free choice to find a more grounded and healthy way of interacting with the world. There is no leap of faith involved; all you have to do is pay attention to your thoughts, then use that awareness in conjunction with REBT to develop a more stable perspective.

Importantly, REBT has benefits beyond treating partisanship. There's a good chance that practicing REBT will help you live a better life, even if partisanship is not creating problems or stress for you. Research suggests that REBT is an effective treatment for anxiety disorders, depression, obsessive compulsive disorder (OCD), and anger management.[108] Moreover, REBT improves both academic and athletic performance, which suggests that its benefits are more far-reaching than any one mental disorder.[109] In short, REBT can help anyone lead a more rational and healthy life.

The ABC Model

As I explained in Chapter 3, partisanship is not inherently negative. Just like anxiety and fear, partisanship becomes unhealthy when it is based on irrational and unrealistic beliefs. In order to cure irrational partisanship, you must identify your irrational perspectives and thought processes and replace them with more accurate perceptions of your situation. Albert Ellis developed the ABC model to identify irrational thinking and replace it with rational perspectives.[110] The basic premise of the ABC model is that the things that happen to us do not cause unhappiness; instead, it's our *perceptions* of what happens in our lives that create unhappiness. By simply finding a new perspective on the events in your life, you can say goodbye to much of your mental anguish.

In the ABC model, activating events (A) lead to consequences (C), and are mediated by our beliefs (B) about those events. The goal of REBT is to focus on the middle part (B) of the equation. Much of the time, A (the activating event) is outside our control. Despite our best efforts, we can't always control what happens around us. A foundational aspect of most major religions is the acknowledgment that we can't control everything, and the resolution to be at peace with that condition. What we can control, however, are the thoughts we carry about those events (B, our beliefs). The beliefs we adopt determine the personal consequences (C) of that event (our emotions and behaviors). This means that our beliefs about the events in our lives influence where our life goes and what new events we're going to face in the future. In other words, it's not what happens to you, it's how you think about what happens to you that determines your experiences in life.

REBT focuses on improving your perspective of your life's events. Whether you have an argument with a family member, lose your job, or watch the other political party win an election, your beliefs about these events will largely determine how you feel and act. Your ability to handle those external events depends on how you perceive them. When you irrationally perceive the significance of the event as greater than it actually is, you'll feel more intense emotions and react to the event in less healthy ways. In contrast, when you hold a more complete and level-headed perspective, you're more likely to respond with a healthy expression of emotions and constructive behaviors. The ultimate aim of REBT is to identify the irrational beliefs that are causing problems in your life, and to replace them with a more accurate and rational perspective. When you practice REBT, you'll find yourself dealing with lower levels of chronic stress, anxiety, depression, addiction, guilt, and anger.

The ABC model can help you overcome irrational beliefs about politics too. In order to gain a more accurate perspective on political situations (and stabilize your emotions), you need to identify the areas where your beliefs about those situations trigger unhelpful reactions and learn to replace them with more useful perspectives. Doing so will change the consequences of those events. In part, this requires us to identify our beliefs about opposing partisans, or expectations about how they should act, and replace them with a more collaborative and non-obsessive approach to their ideas.

Once you replace your irrational beliefs about the opposing party with rational beliefs, your political life will start to shift from unhealthy and ineffective to healthy and constructive.

Unconditional Self-Acceptance

Some of our most irrational beliefs are those we hold about ourselves. When you make a mistake or act badly, you may conclude that you're a bad and awful person. If you don't know something, you might think you're stupid. When other people don't hold you in high regard, you may believe you're worthless. Far too often, we base our self-perceptions on small moments or narrow observations about ourselves. Albert Ellis called this perspective "conditional self-acceptance" because our sense of self-worth requires completely perfect behavior in every situation.

According to Ellis, conditional self-acceptance is unhealthy for a variety of reasons: "First, being a fallible human, you often perform quite badly. Second, even if you perform well at important tasks, many people may choose to dislike you for one reason or another. Third, even if you perform very well and are generally liked by others today, how do you know how successful and well-liked you will be tomorrow? Conditional self-esteem is always—yes, always—in doubt. It causes more anxiety, and more feelings of personal worthlessness, than probably any other aspect of human living."[111]

As an alternative, Ellis proposes a healthier and more rational approach: unconditional self-acceptance (USA). As Ellis argues, "In Rational Emotive Behavior Therapy, we encourage you to refrain from rating your self, your totality, your essence, or your being at all—but instead to rate only your acts, deeds, and performances."[112] To be clear, we need to evaluate ourselves honestly and accurately on specific moments of failure or particular areas of skill. This is what stops me from quitting my job and pursuing an athletic career with the Chicago Cubs. As much as I would love to play for the Cubs, it is very healthy for me to recognize the limitations of my skill in that domain.

The point of USA is not to believe that you're great at everything. Rather, it is to develop a more complex, unique, and comprehensive view of yourself that does not condition your entire self-worth on one particular attribute, skill, moment, or action. Just because I'm not good enough to play professional baseball doesn't mean I'm a worthless human being. Every human has value and worth in their uniqueness, and it's impossible to objectively rate people in their entirety. To do so would require that everyone agree on exactly what skills, behaviors, characteristics, and goals are objectively more important than others.

Some people value money or popularity, others value intelligence, while some believe athletic ability or physical strength are the more important characteristics of a person, and still others value morals and character. Is your babysitter's attentiveness and care more important than your airplane pilot's flying acumen? Is your GP's diagnostic skill more important than your surgeon's competence? Does your favorite musician do more important work than your child's coach? Does the always-smiling disabled man down the street improve your day more than the always-serious power grid manager who keeps your lights running? Which one of those contributions is objectively most important? You may be able to form an opinion on this question, but whatever it is, others are bound to disagree with you (and to have a sound argument for their side).

It makes no sense to think of yourself as a good or bad person, because there are so many attributes to consider and no way of objectively ranking them. Instead, you need to be the best you. Doing one thing poorly doesn't mean that you are worthless, and one mistake doesn't define who you are as a person (nor does one success). Just like everyone else, you have done things you regret, you've accidentally (or even purposefully) hurt others, and you've screwed things up. You may have done a bad thing, but you are not a bad person. Likewise, just because you did a good thing doesn't mean you're a good person—it is unhealthy, unwise, and irrational to think so. Practicing USA means learning to avoid making universal judgments and conclusions about yourself, and to dispute any previous judgments and conclusions you may have made about yourself.

For example, a healthy belief about your poor actions is, "I made a mistake, so I will try to fix it." Just like with anxiety, an appropriate amount of shame, applied in the right way, can be good, healthy, and constructive because it points to something we can do better. Excessive, abusive, or misapplied shame, on the other hand, is dysfunctional, irrational, destructive, and self-defeating. Dragging yourself through the mud and calling yourself "worthless" is unproductive, unhealthy, and likely to result in more bad behavior. You'll make much more progress and do much more good in the world by unconditionally accepting that you are a human being worthy of dignity and respect. As Ellis explains, it is more rational to assess your individual actions in regard to how they're helping you live a productively engaged and happily motivated life:

"You set up your goals and purposes—for example, to remain alive now that you are living and to be happy (to enjoy relatively little pain and much pleasure)—and then you rate or evaluate all your thoughts, feelings, and behaviors *in terms of these goals and purposes.* Thus, you rate your thought "I am a worthwhile person, who deserves to live and enjoy life" as 'good' because it is a thought that helps you stay alive and enjoy life, and you rate your thought "I am a worthless person who deserves to suffer and die" as ‹bad' because it sabotages your purposes. Similarly, you rate your feelings of pleasure in succeeding at a task as 'good' and your displeasure at failing in this task as 'bad' because this mode of thought helps you to be happy. Also, you rate your refraining from overeating as 'good' and your indulging in overeating as 'bad' because such behavior helps you survive and be in good health."[113]

Accept that you are not perfect and never will be. In fact, aiming for perfection is inherently contradictory, because we will never all agree on how someone should behave.

In politics, one particularly problematic irrational belief is that "the other party must not appear to win any debate—they must not hold any credibility, at all. Rather, my party must always show itself superior, must always be in the right." Remember that there's no such thing as perfection within the realm of earthly competence. This error in our political thinking goes further: "If my party's ever wrong or doesn't have all the answers—if I'm wrong in supporting them or in any of my political opinions—then that would imply I'm an ignorant and useless person."

Do you see the shift that just happened from judging one particular act to judging your entire self-worth? We've already discussed how one of the reasons we defend our party is to protect our self-esteem, because if our party is bad, we are bad. But of course, this is ridiculous! You are not your party, and your party is not every argument it puts forward. The party you vote for is just one aspect, one expression, of who you are. Think of all the violent extremists out there who belong to your party. Are they good people just because they vote for the same candidates you do? Your party winning and losing has no reflection on you any more than the success or failure of your favorite sports team. You didn't play in the game, nor did you run for office. If you stop rating yourself, you no longer have to worry about your party losing. But the belief that we need to preserve our own self-esteem may drive us to tear down opposing partisans so we can feel better about ourselves. That derogatory attitude allows us to gloss over our own party's flaws, mistakes, and weaknesses.

Unconditional self-acceptance can also help you recognize the value of your political contribution in a larger context. Do you remember that list of attributes we compared a moment ago (with the babysitter vs. airline pilot, etc.)? Were you able to cleanly rank every single one of them? What if it's the case that the Republican Party and the Democratic Party *both* serve our country equally, though differently (with their commensurate weaknesses alongside their strengths)? What if each expresses different concerns and values that serve us in ways we don't immediately recognize, but that are no less important? What if, instead of defensively comparing ourselves against one another, we instead choose to accept that their value doesn't take away from our own value and that we actually need both? USA can help facilitate everyday political discussions—and all discussions, for that matter—by making you generally less defensive when you may be wrong or ignorant about something. You just need to put your ego aside and stop caring if you're right or wrong.

Another great tool to become less defensive in difficult moments is self-affirmation. Self-affirmation can improve the way you see yourself, and therefore make you less defensive when you face a disagreement. Simply think of something you do well or something you like about yourself. When someone challenges your beliefs, think of things you're good at, people you've helped, or contributions you've made to the world. For example, if you read a social media post that challenges your opinion on some topic, remind yourself that you're a good spouse, parent, or friend. Think of the good you do through your job, volunteer work, or the half marathon you ran last month. Self-affirmation gives you permission to be wrong and possibly lose face in this particular situation. When that happens, you'll feel less need to defend yourself, your political beliefs, or the positions of others in your political party.

People find it more acceptable to admit their party made a mistake when they do not believe the party is fundamental to their identity or essential to their sense of self-esteem. In other words, reminding yourself that there's more to life than party identification decreases irrational partisanship. In contrast, obsessing over political arguments or forgetting that there's more to you than the candidate you support will make you defensive of your political party and lead you down the path of irrationality. When your sense of self-worth is tied up in your party identification, any threat to the party becomes a personal threat to you. You can untangle your self-worth from your political opinions by shifting your focus with self-affirmations like, "I'm proud to be an open-minded person who listens to others without judging them."

Unconditional self-acceptance is a powerful long-term strategy that will help you in both political and non-political ways, but note that it will take time for you to practice USA and to question all your irrational beliefs that lead you to take things personally. Self-affirmation is a particularly useful tool to use just before entering a potentially difficult conversation, or when your party loses an election or policy battle. When you begin to feel defensiveness creeping in, simply review other aspects of your daily life—particularly those moments when you did something meaningful and positive for someone else. This can help you shift your thoughts and your emotions so you can better relate to yourself and others.

Unconditional Other Acceptance

If it's irrational to judge your entire self, then it stands to reason that you also shouldn't make sweeping judgements of others when they fail to behave as you think they should. As Ellis puts it, "In plain English, [unconditional other acceptance] means accepting the sinner but not the sin. So when people act immorally, unethically, or badly to you (and others), you observe their thoughts, emotions, and deeds, tentatively judge that they are 'improper' and 'wrong,' but rigorously refrain from rating them as a whole . . . as bad, wrong, or inept people."[114]

Essentially, unconditional other acceptance stems from the Golden Rule ("treat others as you want to be treated"). Would you like others to judge you entirely based on your partisanship? Does that encompass the totality of who you are as a human being? Of course not. When you provide UOA, you're demonstrating that it's okay for other people to make mistakes or do things differently than you do, and it's more likely they will provide the same grace to you.

People are so varied and have so many different features that it is foolish to judge them based on how they voted or how their values differ from yours. In fact, you can't reliably judge any individual based on any group they belong to. Are you constantly thinking about partisanship and politics in your daily life? Is it the driver of all your day-to-day decisions? I certainly hope not! And it isn't for those in the other party either. Politics is a small part of most people's lives. Republicans volunteer and donate to charities, just like Democrats. Democrats care about the legacy they leave behind them, just like Republicans. And some members of both parties slack off, make excuses, and break laws. There isn't much difference between how opposing partisans spend their time, but there's a huge difference between individuals within each one of the parties.

The lesson? Don't judge a person on one single characteristic or opinion that has little to do with the fullness of who they are and what they contribute.

Perhaps UOA seems too much of a stretch for you. Although it might be a great strategy for dealing with most people, you might find that one guy who can't stop talking about conspiracy theories unforgivable. If you can't find a way to unconditionally accept someone, a quick and easy alternative is to focus on their non-political (or non-annoying) characteristics. Instead of fixating on what they said that annoyed you, take a deep breath and make a point to look for their other non-political characteristics of value.

When I moved into my house a few years ago, my next-door neighbor was the first person to welcome me to the neighborhood. Ever since, he and his wife have been friendly and helpful and have even delighted in watching my son grow up over the years. They've been nothing but nice, decent people for the entire time we've known them. A few months prior to the 2020 election, they posted yard signs supporting candidates that my wife and I didn't support. For over five years, we had considered them good, kind-hearted people, but now, we started to feel negatively toward them simply because we learned of their party identification. Did they all of a sudden become bad neighbors? Were they bad people now? Nothing had changed, except that it was a highly-charged political environment, which led me to prioritize their party identification when I looked at them, rather than the countless other times they had been kind and helpful.

Let's consider how the ABC framework can be used to understand events like this. The activating event— my neighbor's yard sign—was outside my control. I chose at first to focus my attention on my negative universal judgments of the opposing political party. The consequence was that I felt more angry and distrusting of my neighbors. Those consequences were a result of the beliefs I chose to adopt and focus on.

I hope you can see how ridiculous I was being. Now, I intentionally didn't tell you what party they belong to, because that would bias your interpretation of whether my reaction was fair, appropriate, and healthy. It wasn't, period!

It really doesn't matter what party we belong to, because it is unwise and unhealthy to judge anyone based on their party identification. If your friends, family, neighbors, coworkers, or potential employers concluded that you're a bad person and started to view you negatively just because you vote for one party over the other, where would that lead? Unless you'd like to see more of that kind of behavior in the world (on both sides of the political spectrum), then don't propagate that behavior. Don't let a person's party identification affect your judgment of them. All I had to do to rekindle the good feelings I used to have about my neighbors was change my focus to all the kind things they've done for my family and me over the years instead of focusing on their political signs.

The good-vs-evil narrative that predominates

western culture makes it hard for most people to adopt a UOA mindset. Consider the basic theme of the most popular movies year after year: the protagonist is morally upstanding, though they may have superficial flaws, while the antagonist is morally corrupted by some extreme ideology and has zero compassion for others. The hero kills the villain and his henchman to claim victory and save the world. One important part of the narrative is that the "evil" bad guys deserve to die. (If they didn't, these movies would not be nearly as popular.) The bad guys must be seen as deserving of death and suffering because they have sinned or acted in some fundamentally immoral and inhuman way. Only then can we righteously cheer their deaths and leave the movie theater with a warm, fuzzy feeling that justice was served and all is once again right in the world.

One problem with this narrative is that no one ever thinks of themselves as the villain. From our own perspective, we each perceive ourselves through the lens of our intentions, so we conclude that we're generally doing good in the world. We are all the heroes of our own stories, the centers of our own universes. But since we often misinterpret other people's intentions (because we can never actually know what they are without asking), we often judge others as "bad" when they make the very same mistakes we often make.

Another problem is that reality is much more complicated than the plot line for *Spiderman* might lead you to believe. One reason why you may see your political interactions with others as morally clear is that you're interpreting the real world through the simplified narrative of good vs. evil. When you experience reality, your brain naturally wants to identify the protagonist (usually you) and the antagonist (someone not in your group or tribe), even if it's not really an appropriate distinction for the circumstances. Once you think of someone as a hero or a villain, it's hard for you to shift that mindset. The mind automatically engages in this dichotomous good/bad thinking, so to some extent this is out of your control. Your mind also biases your interpretations of all the other events connected to that person once you've labeled them as either good or bad. That's why it can help to consciously focus your mind on people's good qualities so you can retrain your mind instead of being driven only by the good/bad narrative.

Separate Needs from Wants

One of the most common ways we develop irrational beliefs is by losing sight of our real situation and turning our wants into needs. A central aim of REBT is learning to more accurately identify the things we need in our lives and distinguish them from the things we want. It's not that our wants are necessarily unimportant, but the distinction between needs and wants is very important.

The things you ultimately need comprise a very short list: food, water, basic shelter, clothing, one or two close relationships, and occasional health care. These things alone will get you most of the way to a deeply rewarding life. Most other things in our lives are simply wants: an impressive education, a smart phone, a job we love, a large television, and lots of friends who think we're awesome. But you don't need any of that to survive or live a healthy life. While this might seem obvious, many of us have mistaken our wants for our needs, and this error causes many of our other dysfunctions and irrational behaviors.

When we treat our wants like needs, we can become anxious, fearful, or angry whenever circumstances don't unfold the way we want them to. This is particularly true when it comes to social acceptance or esteem. You may want the people around you to think highly of you, to view you as smart, talented, or good-looking. It certainly seems like it would be nice if everyone thought all those positive things about you and never rolled their eyes when you talked, became frustrated with you, or disparaged you to others. But you don't need the esteem of others, and it's not the end of the world if somebody somewhere doesn't think you're amazing.

Similarly, we don't need others to treat us the way we think we deserve to be treated. As Ellis explains, "People, to be sure, often cheat you, assault you, and go back on their promises to you. So, almost instantly, you become disappointed and displeased about their actions. But when you are angry, you go beyond that disappointment and displeasure to feelings of rage by insisting that the people who make you angry absolutely must not be the way they are and must not do the things that they do. It is your grandiose insistence that they behave 'properly' and 'fairly' that creates your anger—and not their poor behavior" (emphasis added).[115] When we allow our wants to become needs, we lose sight of our ability to find satisfaction in an imperfect world.

It is important to accept the fact that you cannot personally eradicate all the injustice in the world. If that statement shocks you, well, welcome to the real world—this realization is an important part of maturing, interacting with others like an adult, and finally making a real positive difference in the world. Death, sickness, and unfair luck are an inevitable part of life, but that's OK. Despite the pain and struggle, life can still bring beauty and joy.

Let's take a simple example: I have a soft spot for animals, and I hate that some people abuse and neglect them. Every time I see a commercial from the ASPCA with shivering cold dogs and scared cats, it hurts my conscience, along with my heart. If I could, I would stop all animal suffering, but I simply can't. Instead, I try to do what I can, like donate to the ASPCA and adopt five rescue cats into my home (yes, I'm *that* crazy cat guy). I wish our government would provide more funding for animal shelters and impose stricter penalties on animal abusers, but even if that were to happen, there would always be animals suffering in the world. I recognize that I don't need to (and can't) stop all animal abuse, and that's why it doesn't consume my entire life.

There are many injustices in the world, but we each must recognize that there is no such thing as perfect solutions to complex problems. And we should recognize that each little action we take does make a difference, even if we can't eradicate animal abuse, poverty, or long lines at the grocery store. If we accept that perfection is not a viable option, then we can accept that life can still be wonderful in the midst of that imperfection. We have to stop thinking that the world absolutely must be fair, just, and free of any suffering in order for anything to be good. Our life can be great just the way it is right now, once we choose to let go of the belief we need to get all our wants fulfilled.

Would it be nice if the world were a perfectly comfortable and fair place? Some philosophers think that might actually be torture for humans, because we need goals and things to work toward. Regardless, you'll drive yourself crazy if you expect the world to be whatever your definition of "perfect" is. The world is what it is; you can choose to accept things as they are, or you can choose to be unhappy until you get what you want. You must accept that all people are never going to act exactly the way you think they should and that there will always be suffering, murder, and innocent deaths.

The same lesson applies to every political issue, whether it's abortion, climate change, or immigration. It would be wonderful if your issue of choice were completely and permanently resolved in the way you think it should be, but the world is much bigger than you are, and there's only so much you can do. Even if you succeed in a small way, suffering will absolutely still exist, in one form or another. When you believe that your political policy of choice must become law (or that another policy must not), you make the mistake of believing your want is a need, and that mistake will interfere with your ability to live a happy and healthy life. You don't need the world to change to be happy—you just need to let go of thinking the world has to be a certain way.

Don't get me wrong: you should fight to make the world a better place—but it's counterproductive to agonize about your issue of choice, to lose sleep because the world's not perfect, or to hate people who may be concerned about other injustices or suffering more than the thing you're most concerned about. If you can accept that other people have different priorities about how to make the world a better place and that they may have a good reason to disagree with your particular solution , you're setting yourself up to be a lot less stressed and a lot more open-minded.

In sum, REBT is uniquely suited to address our problems with irrational partisanship: its simplicity and easy application, combined with the fact that it directly attacks the roots of irrational behavior, make it an ideal solution for our cultural situation. REBT's ABC model helps us reinterpret events and circumstances in constructive, forward-moving ways. USA helps us find emotional stability and self-confidence, which makes us less defensive and more capable of engaging productively with others and with life's challenges. And UOA puts our interactions with others in a larger context, which reminds us to pause before making sweeping judgements based on just a single characteristic, like their party affiliation. Most importantly of all, REBT teaches us to distinguish between rational and irrational beliefs, reasonable and unreasonable expectations, and to keep wants and needs in proper perspective.

Treatment: Negative Visualization

One quick and easy way to improve your perspective is to practice negative visualization. To do so, simply think about the things you value most in your life, such as your spouse, children, job, home, friends, financial security, or the food in your fridge. Then imagine what life would be like without those things. We often lose sight of the fact that what we have can be taken away at any moment without warning. Your loved ones can die suddenly; you can suffer a catastrophic injury; your spouse can leave you; your home could burn to the ground. How would you feel if you no longer had those things? This thought experiment can help you find gratitude for the gifts you currently have, and let go of all the other things that just don't matter.

Negative visualization can also help reduce anger and anxiety. The world can be a scary place when we let ourselves get carried away thinking there's something awfully wrong with it just because it's not exactly the way we want it to be. If we allow our wants to become needs, we get stuck in irrational thinking and painful emotions. That's when we lose sight of our ability to find satisfaction in our imperfect world, and so cease to move forward at all.

Now write down the things that you care about most in this world. Imagine if those things were taken from you. How petty would political disputes seem if you lost those things? Would you trade any of those things for your party to win the next election? You may want your party to win and the other party to lose, but would your life be ruined if the other party won? Was your life ruined the last time the opposing party won an election?

CHAPTER 9

How Partisan Media Sell Hate and Fear

"The implied objective of this line of thought is a nightmare world in which the Leader, or some ruling clique, controls not only the future but the past. If the Leader says of such and such an event, "It never happened"—well, it never happened. If he says that two and two are five—well, two and two are five."

—George Orwell

I have journeyed from the extreme right to the radical left, and now reside firmly in a world of political ambivalence. My time as a Republican taught me the importance of listening to people who are socially, culturally, and ideologically different. My time as a Democrat taught me an important lesson about the real power of partisan media in generating hatred across the country.

During my days as a radical Democrat, I spent a lot of time watching MSNBC and reading liberal blogs. Although the Iraq War was the initial impetus for my switch to the Democratic Party, I didn't start disliking Republicans until I made Air America and Countdown with Keith Olbermann a regular part of my news diet. In 2004, I commuted between my home in Golden, Colorado and my school in Laramie, Wyoming. In case you're unfamiliar with that region, that's a very long, though very beautiful, drive to make in one day. And for most of the five hours a day I spent in the car, I listened to Air America, because they were funny and the hosts reflected my liberal views. Upon my arrival home, I would watch Hardball with Chris Matthews and Countdown with Keith Olbermann.

Looking back, the main attraction of these partisan media programs was not so much that they told me I was right. The main appeal was their demonization of George W. Bush and of the Republicans who supported him. They framed the world as good vs. bad, where Democrats had figured things out and were on the side of the good, while clueless, immoral Republicans were the ones screwing everything up and getting in the way of what could otherwise be a thriving country. Since I identified as a Democrat, this made me feel good about myself—I felt superior and self-righteous, at least compared to the ignorant, heartless, and corrupt Republicans. I was among the heroes in the story, while Republicans were the villains. Of course, I conveniently forgot that I was a member of the villains just a short time ago. No matter, now I was on the side of righteousness!

Liberal partisan programs presented facts and events in such a way that implied any intelligent, moral, honest human could recognize that one side was obviously right: the Democrats. George W. Bush was a heartless, racist President who cared nothing for all the soldiers and innocent civilians he killed. Republican congresspeople knew he was wrong, but supported him anyway because they were cowards. And because the facts so clearly favored Democrats, Republican voters could only be stupid and immoral.

This is what liberal media led me to believe, and I am now proud to say that I was wrong.

When I stopped paying attention to liberal media, something amazing happened in my life: I slowly started to feel less anger and hatred toward Republicans. Moreover, my political conversations with them became much more engaging and constructive. It was a long recovery period that eventually resulted in my declaration as an Independent voter shortly after I wrote *Disagreeing Agreeably*. My big takeaway from that experience is that liberal media did not deepen my political insight at all. Instead, it simply made me hate people who didn't share my pre-existing views.

Conservative news programs do the same thing for Republican partisans. That's how partisan media outlets make money and foster political hatred among their audiences. Partisan media fuel your ego, making you feel self-righteous and intellectually superior to the other party. When you're watching or listening to a partisan media program, it's easy to convince yourself that you're just getting the news of the day. But in reality, the programs are merely fattening you up on sweet-tasting (though self-destructive) validation. The more these biased media personalities can get you to feel angry and afraid of the other party, the better you'll feel about your current political beliefs and opinions. And the more fear, anger, and validation you feel, the more you'll watch, and the more money they earn from advertising. They're selling the same good vs. evil story that Hollywood does, but in a much more manipulative way!

Recall that your unconscious mind remembers which experiences have made you happy and which ones made you unhappy. If a particular news program makes you feel happy with validation, you will unconsciously seek to re-experience that happiness, even if you are unaware of exactly what it was about the experience that you liked.

As a comparison, imagine that I spiked your soda with a small amount of cocaine without your knowing. As you drink the soda, you would feel the chemical boost that comes with cocaine, feeling happier and more energetic without really knowing why. But your mind would unconsciously associate that particular beverage with the pleasant feelings that came from the drug. Meanwhile, you won't feel the negative effects of withdrawal until sometime later, and your mind will not associate those feelings with the drink. The next time you choose a drink, you might select the same soda in search of that good feeling. If I asked you why you picked that one over all the others, you would probably rationalize your choice, saying something like, "I've always loved this soda," or, "It's a good price." Really though, you were motivated to choose that drink because your unconscious mind remembered its appeal from your last positive experience with it. Likewise, people choose partisan media programs, at least in part, because those programs have made them feel happy in the past. They will justify it by telling themselves and others that "they're more accurate" or "other news outlets are biased"—but those are just rationalizations. Just as alcoholics, chain smokers, and compulsive gamblers rationalize their "innocent" behavior, partisans convince themselves of their preferred station's reliability and authority, when in fact they're just addicted to feeling like the heroes in a story of good vs. evil.

Many mental illnesses begin simply as small habits

and continue to ratchet upward until they've become destructive compulsions. For many people, turning to like-minded media is a seemingly harmless habit that has become reinforced over time. The problem is that partisan media deliver content that makes partisans more likely to only seek news sources that confirm their pre-existing opinions and suspicions. You tune in to Sean Hannity one day and hear his take on the immoral Democrats who actively hate America, the righteous conservative Republicans who resist them and won't fall for their tactics and lies, and all about how "we're going to save the country!" This makes you feel good about yourself for seeing the truth of the matter, so now you're motivated and energized to do something about the problem. It fuels your ego and gives you purpose. After all, who doesn't want to think of themselves as one of the good guys making the world a better place? It fits into the Hollywood narrative that we've been fed our entire lives.

This neurochemical surge (i.e., the good feeling) acts as a reward, similar to the high a gambler feels after a big win. Your mind then unconsciously seeks to re-experience that reward and will constantly seek to spend more time listening to your favorite news and talk radio hosts. All the while, being frequently exposed to the shallow bashing of the other party manipulates your emotions, which builds an intense storm of self-righteous anger aimed directly at the opposing party's members. In this way, partisan media outlets are like drug dealers: they get you hooked by chemically manipulating your feel-good brain and boosting your ego. You tune in more often to get your fix of the drug, which boosts ratings for the most incendiary and uncivil programs. As those programs make more money, other struggling or startup businesses imitate their model. Partisan media gain more status and make more money the more they embroil you in their narrow-sighted hatred of opposing partisans.

The more you watch and listen, the more addicted you become.

Making matters worse, the more attention you pay to partisan media, the more biased it makes mainstream outlets appear by comparison. As a result, you come to believe that only your favorite self-validating media voices are telling the truth, since every time you change the channel, the opinions you hear are so radically different because you've swung from one extremely biased source to another on the opposite end of the spectrum. Eventually, you are only getting news from sources that demonize opposing partisans, because by comparison all other media appear biased. The more time you spend in your partisan media echo chamber, the more distorted your perception becomes.

There is plenty of research verifying this dangerous effect of partisan media. My own research has shown that watching partisan cable news outlets, such as Fox News and MSNBC, makes people more negative toward leaders in the opposing party.[116] Partisan media can even cause internal party divisions during contentious presidential primaries.[117] Other research indicates that partisan media intensifies hostility toward opposing partisans and reduces support for legislative compromise.[118] There is also evidence that partisan media focus more attention on the issues that their viewers want to see—not necessarily on the questions and topics that matter most.[119] That is, partisan media conduct market research and learn that their partisan viewers care about some political issues more than others. The networks then focus their attention on those issues, rather than the events and topics that are actually affecting your life in meaningful ways. As a result, their viewers or listeners increasingly come to live in an echo chamber where they only hear about the problems they want to hear about, in the way they want to hear about them. As such, they no longer need to hear opposing arguments or think about issues that make them uncomfortable. Partisan media make billions of dollars by brainwashing Americans into thinking there is only one correct viewpoint on every issue and that you should hate anyone who disagrees with your views.

Ongoing exposure to partisan media gives the listener comfort by selling the story of good vs. evil and only providing evidence and arguments that fit that narrative. Unfortunately, it's a false representation of the real world. This divorce of perception from reality can have deeply destructive outcomes, as we've discussed previously. Accepting this alternate reality will inevitably lead to self-defeating behaviors, which include making poor decisions, ending valuable relationships, and putting yourself (and others) at unnecessary risk. Above all, the most deeply dangerous aspect of partisan media is the effect it has on our perceptions of, and feelings toward, opposing partisans. Partisan media creates the feeling that those in the other party are clueless and blind, heartless and power-hungry, and/or extremists and raging ideologues.

One of the most insidious tactics that partisan media employ to this end is providing "exemplars" of the opposing party. An exemplar is simply a person that supposedly represents the entire party in a nutshell. Partisan media focus their attention on the most ridiculous, extreme, and scary members of the opposing party, and then use them as exemplars to stand in for all members of the opposing party. This is an important sleight of hand to recognize. There are extreme, uncompromising fringe groups in both political parties who actively promote hatred and violence. If you think your party doesn't, then you aren't looking hard enough. (For proof, check out the map of hate groups maintained by the Southern Poverty Law Center, last updated to reflect 2020 data. You can find it at www. splcenter.org/hate-map.[120]) When partisan media direct their audience's attention to these extreme exemplars, they paint a picture of the other party as radical and threatening. Repeated exposure to partisan media leaves Democrats believing Republicans are all racist morons, and Republicans thinking Democrats hate America and hold no respect for anything sacred—neither of which is true for the vast majority of Democrats and Republicans.

There is plenty of evidence that partisan media play a leading role in demonizing both leaders and members of the opposing party. According to a recent study, nearly all partisans believe members of the other party are brainwashed and hateful.[121] Specifically, 88 percent of Democrats believe Republicans are brainwashed, while 86 percent of Republicans say the same about Democrats. Nearly equal portions of Democrats (87 percent) and Republicans (84 percent) believe the other party is hateful. And while 89 percent of Democrats think Republicans are racist, 71 percent of Republicans say the same about Democrats. Although partisan media are not entirely responsible for this, they are certainly a pivotal player.

The same study also examined Americans' perceptions of the views their opposing partisans hold, and then compared them to the actual views held by real-life members of each party. The study found that exposure to partisan media increased misperceptions of the extremeness of political opponents. In fact, those who got their news from partisan media were the most likely of any group to overestimate the extremeness of opposing partisans. Conversely, those getting most of their news from broadcast television (ABC, CBS, and NBC) held more accurate perceptions of Democrats' and Republicans' actual standing on political issues. In fact, those getting their political information from broadcast news sources were the only ones with roughly accurate perceptions of the American political divide.[122]

So if you're tired of the lunacy and extremism that seems to be all around, or if you have any desire to be impartial and fair in your assessments of political situations, then avoid partisan news. Abandon these manipulators and opt for non-partisan news sources instead. Partisan media do you no good and slowly ruin your life.

The Game Frame

Although, better, mainstream media still aren't perfect. While mainstream media may be less blatantly self-gratifying and narrow-sighted than partisan media, they still uphold and fuel irrational partisanship, albeit in a more subtle way.

In the late twentieth century, journalists and pundits began to intentionally adopt a style for presenting political information, which has become known as the "game frame." In the game frame, political events are presented as a zero-sum competition, like a two-team sport, in which the two parties compete to win elections.[123] In this frame, opinion polls are the scoreboard, and elections are the ultimate battlefield. Journalist and so-called experts now discuss political events almost exclusively through this game frame, and give us their play-by-play commentary on which party won or lost the news cycle. Watch national news even a little and you will see how prominent this game framing is in media coverage. Those who pay the most attention to this coverage inevitably absorb this perspective, and as a result become fans of their team (party), rather than citizens and neighbors in their country.

An alternative way to present political events is to simply report the strongest arguments surrounding each event (which, by the way, means that there will be more than two)—again, unfiltered. Unfortunately, this approach is not very exciting. But when news was intended to inform rather than entertain, this was precisely how news programs discussed national politics. Journalists let politicians speak; they created an open space for key players in the policy process to express their arguments, and they trusted the public to take personal ownership of their own thoughts, make critical evaluations, and then make up their own minds.

However, growth demands—along with competition from cable news, talk radio, and the internet—put pressure on all news outlets to present political happenings in a more entertaining, triggering, and attention-grabbing way. Decision makers in the news outlets understood that policy details were some of the least interesting content.

But they saw that viewers did get hooked by sports and competition. It didn't take long for them to realize that framing the political landscape as if it were a sport would capture more attention and emotional engagement from the viewing public. As news outlets across the ideological spectrum began to frame politics as a two-team sport, Americans started to see politics as a duopoly and competition, rather than a discussion about how we should govern the country. People became more interested in which party would win the next election than who had the best ideas or what challenges people actually faced. It all became about winning!

Research even shows that poll coverage is the most popular type of coverage in the news media, while issue coverage is the least popular.[124] In other words, people are more concerned with who is winning or losing than they are with what is currently being done or what the winning candidate would actually do. Our attention has been shifted away from the behaviors of politicians that truly influence our lives, and now we mostly focus on who's winning and losing. The fallacy of this situation is that politics isn't about who's winning or losing—it's about which decisions our elected officials are making, and which decisions we want them to make. The entire perspective peddled by the news media is false and misrepresents reality.

Even mainstream media continue to feed us with a false game frame. Personally, I turn the channel and don't bother reading any articles about who's winning or losing in the polls. We will find out who won after the election. To constantly check the polls is a pathetic waste of your time, but the media focus on it because it's easy and emotionally triggering, and because irrational partisans care about it enough to regularly pay attention to it, which boosts the news source's profits.

If we cured partisanship, Americans wouldn't care about who's winning, or about what percentages of Americans believe this or have fallen for that. Then the media could stop covering the horse race and instead focus on candidates' specific concerns, issue positions, and qualifications—you know, the stuff that actually matters!

Perceptions of Media Bias

Perhaps you believe that a particular partisan media outlet is the only news source you can trust to report the news accurately. You may believe the mainstream outlets are politically biased against your party. Well, I hate to break it to you, but you are an absolutely terrible judge of media bias. I don't mean you in particular—it's that all humans are bad at judging media bias. We all suffer from personal biases that make it nearly impossible to accurately judge political bias in news sources. Our perceptions of media bias are more a reflection of our own beliefs than they are of any actual media biases.[125] When a news source is truly balanced or objective, Democrats will think it favors Republicans, while Republicans will believe it favors Democrats—even when the news report is exactly the same! This is similar to the phenomenon where fans of opposing sports teams each think the referees favored the other team during the exact same game.[126] Our evaluations of media bias are colored by our own biases; if the media were to simply present arguments fairly and accurately, without taking sides, most of us would still think they are biased because we tend to perceive our side's views as the absolute truth, while any information that doesn't fit our current worldview is untrustworthy.

If you've ever felt that the media is biased against your views, you're not alone. Accusations of political bias in the American news media are as old as the country. Following the Revolutionary War, party-run newspapers would brazenly attack the policies and personal lives of opposing party leaders or candidates, such as John Adams and Thomas Jefferson. In fact, anger over perceived media bias drove John Adams to sign the Alien and Sedition Act, which allowed the government to jail newspaper editors for publishing negative news about the government and— in particular, about the president. That's right, newspaper publishers could be sent to jail (and were) for criticizing the president of the United States.

Since then, there have been numerous other notable attacks on the media for supposed political bias, such as during the Red Scare, McCarthyism, the Vietnam War, Watergate, and the Iraq War. Presidents of both parties— including Lyndon Johnson, Richard Nixon, Ronald Reagan, George H. W. Bush, Bill Clinton, George W. Bush, Barack Obama, and Donald Trump—have made attacking and de-legitimizing the media a key political strategy at times. You may have noticed that I just named the last six presidents! That's because every recent president has accused media outlets of political bias, though some presidents talked about media bias more than others.

Frequent attacks on the news media have undermined the credibility of mainstream news sources while increasing the influence of partisan news outlets. Many people nowadays think, "If the whole industry is corrupt, then I may as well rely on the people who are telling me what I already know to be true!" As my own research has shown, when politicians accuse the media of political bias, it consistently increases the public's perceptions of bias, regardless of any actual bias in the media.[127] In other words, when politicians say the media are biased, their supporters are likely to believe them on their authority ("they must know more about this than I do!"), even in the cases when no political bias exists.

A Better Standard for Media Bias

How do we know when the media are biased? The most commonly used standard is balanced coverage to each political party. This standard pushes journalists to report "straight down the middle" and to avoid taking sides. The assumption underlying this view is that both parties are equally good and bad. Neither party is objectively right or wrong in any situation. Any time a journalist says something negative about one party, they feel compelled to say something negative about the other party, thus creating an equivalency between the two parties.

Unfortunately, the balance standard is a false equivalency that distorts reality for audiences. Imagine a scenario where all Democratic leaders say that 2+2=5, but Republicans disagree, saying that 2+2=4. If we hold the news media to the balance standard in this scenario, then they would be prohibited from expressing any judgment of validity in the disagreement, and should instead present both claims as equally valid. If journalists correctly said, "Although Democratic party leaders say 2+2=5, they are wrong because when we take two things and then add two more things, there are four things," irrational Democrats would accuse the media of bias in favor of Republicans. They would say, "Who are you to take sides in this debate?" Eventually, Democrats might then form their own partisan media outlets that confidently discuss how our country should respond to the fact that 2+2=5, while avoiding those "biased" outlets that weren't balanced toward their party.

This balance standard assumes that there is no actual reality or true facts, that all opinions are equal even when they are proven false. We would have to assume that there is a Democratic reality and a Republican reality, with no objective way to determine whether either party is right or wrong. Of course, we all know that not every statement is equally valid and true. While political challenges do call for collaboration and debate, that doesn't mean that every argument put forward is a strong one, nor does it mean that all information is equally valid.

There is a better standard for judging political bias in the news media. Consider the example of a baseball umpire calling balls and strikes. If an umpire calls more strikes for one team than another, does that mean the ump must be biased? Of course not! Maybe one team's pitchers are better able to locate the strike zone. But the balance standard would require that umpires call an equal number of strikes for both teams, regardless of where the pitches actually land in relation to the strike zone. Is that an acceptable standard for umpires? No, it's absolutely ridiculous. And it is equally ridiculous to hold the media to the same standard. If a political actor acts poorly, presents a weaker argument, endangers the country's citizens, or tells outright lies, it would be irresponsible of the media to politely condone the behavior without challenging it.

What do we expect of umpires when they call balls and strikes? Or of any referees for that matter? We expect fairness, but not fairness in outcomes—that would mean calling an equal number of balls and strikes for each team, regardless of where their pitches land. A more reasonable standard is to expect that umpires apply the same strike zone to both teams. Fairness requires consistency in the standards of evaluation. If an umpire allotted a larger strike zone for one team while giving a pass to the other team for the exact same types of throws, they would rightly be accused of bias.

Consistency is a more reasonable standard to apply to the media, politicians, and every human being. If one party acts poorly, journalists should point it out. And that goes for everyone: call balls and strikes as you see them, and don't worry about "balancing" both sides or hurting one party's feelings. As long as we establish consistent standards and apply them equally to everyone, regardless of political affiliation, we are behaving in a way that's fair and reasonable. Consistency in standards is very important. Imagine if your boss punished you for doing the exact same things all your other coworkers did. You would rightly complain that it was unfair. When we cling to our irrational partisan perspectives, we stop holding the media accountable for applying consistent standards, and instead reward the media for consistently favoring our party.

Journalists have no choice but to establish their own standards based on their best judgment and professional experience. We all must do so. The key is that, whatever those standards are, we must firmly hold all politicians, political groups, and individuals to those standards on an equal level, consistently over time—even when it's unpleasant to do so. This is what we expect of umpires, judges, and all public servants. To the best of your ability, you must define the standards that you think are most critical to the situation and be consistent in applying them, regardless of who you're dealing with.

Treatment: Focus on Rational Media

Partisans should avoid partisan media outlets for the same reasons that drug addicts should avoid drug dealers, alcoholics should avoid bars, and gamblers should avoid casinos. Avoiding junk media from partisan channels is one of the most important treatment steps for recovery. You should also avoid poll coverage in favor of specific detail coverage.

Instead of focusing on who's winning or losing, focus on the issues, your values, and creating a fair and reasonable standard which you apply to all media and political leaders. Partisan media feed the addiction of irrational partisans by painting a picture of the world where their group is superior and always right. Paying attention to partisan media may make you feel like you're right, but only by warping your reality and distorting your perspective of the other party. Partisan media is like a hallucinogen that leads to delusions of grandeur and makes us hate half the country. Partisan media provide the drug, and partisans are the addicts.

So, what can we do to break free? To be clear, I'm not suggesting that you avoid all news about politics. There are plenty of news outlets available that will inform you about politics without blinding and brainwashing you into hating half the country. Although mainstream news sources are not perfect, they are much better than partisan media and can make you more politically informed and motivated to participate in political affairs. Just as important, mainstream media can make you feel less hostility toward opposing partisans. My own research shows that those who watch broadcast television news on ABC, CBS, NBC, or PBS feel and behave less negatively toward the opposing party compared to those who rely on partisan programming.[128]

Mainstream media can de-escalate political hostility by challenging viewers' stereotypes of opposing partisans. Note that that mainstream news does not have much effect on your actual political views or voting decisions, and contrary to Republican criticisms, mainstream news programs don't make viewers more liberal or more likely to vote for Democrats. Instead, when partisans hear strong arguments from both parties, they simply feel less animosity toward the other party because they can understand the real rationales behind opposing perspectives. Partisans generally come away from a mainstream news broadcast still believing that their party is right, but with the understanding that the opposing party also has a reasonable perspective that is based on values we all share. They may still disagree with each other, but they see that the other party makes some good points and is not completely ignorant or evil after all.

Furthermore, if you want more in-depth discussions of political issues, I encourage you to seek out ideological media outlets instead of partisan media. What's the difference?

Partisan media outlets frame political issues as Democrat vs. Republican, regardless of the value-based underpinnings of a particular issue or event. Ideological media, on the other hand, may align more with one party than another, but they are more concerned with broader policy implications than they are with electoral outcomes. Partisan media attack the other party, while ideological media focus on underlying ideas and policy debates. It's pretty easy to tell the difference between partisan media and ideological media just by looking at their headlines. While partisan media tend to focus on why one party is better than the other, ideological media discuss policy issues and mention political parties only in regard to the policies they support.

Partisan media outlets promote the electoral interests of their political party regardless of what issues or solutions the party is promoting or how dangerous their specific actions may be to the country. In contrast, ideological media only support a party when it acts in accordance with their ideological principles. Any time a party or its leaders violate those principles, ideological media will criticize them, regardless of how this could impact elections or party status.

While partisan media represent the epitome of irrational partisanship, ideological media generally promote rational partisanship, where principles and specific ideas are more important than who wins a particular election. For reference, I've included a list of news outlets categorized as partisan, ideological, and mainstream below. These categories are based on empirical research into media bias, the outlets' explicitly stated missions, and my own judgment.

Try to avoid the outlets labeled "partisan media" below in favor of ideological or mainstream news outlets. Again, the point here is not that non-partisan media are objective or unbiased. Instead, the goal is to avoid the demonization of one party for the self-aggrandizement of the other. Deny yourself the drug that partisan media push and see how quickly your hatred toward the opposing party starts to fade. Give it a try for one month and then retake the survey from the end of Chapter 6 to see if your fear and hatred of the other party has dissipated. My guess is you will see positive results in a short period of time.

Personally, I quit partisan media cold turkey years ago and I haven't regretted it for a second. In fact, I doubt I would have written this book if had I kept getting my fix.

Partisan Media

Breitbart	CNN	Conservative Talk Radio
Daily Kos	Fox News	MSNBC
Newsmax	OAN	The Nation

Ideological Media

American Enterprise Institute	The Atlantic	Brookings Institute
National Review	New York Times	New Yorker
Washington Post	Vice News	Wall Street Journal

Mainstream Media

ABC	BBC	CBS
C-Span	NBC	Newsy
PBS	Politico	Roll Call
USA Today	The Hill	

CHAPTER 10

Changing the System to Cure Partisanship

"The alternate domination of one faction over another; sharpened by the spirit of revenge, natural to party dissension; which in different ages and countries has perpetrated the most horrid enormities, is itself a frightful despotism[…] sooner or later the chief of some prevailing faction more able or more fortunate than his competitors, turns this disposition to the purposes of his own elevation, on the ruins of Public Liberty."

—George Washington, in his *Farewell Address*

George Washington is my favorite president for many reasons, not least of which is his opposition to political parties. In his farewell address, Washington issued a dire and prescient warning about the dangers of political parties. He understood how allegiance to one's party over the country can give way to dictatorship. It's a scary thought, but we may be approaching such a precarious point.

When partisanship dictates our principles instead of reflecting them, it's only a matter of time before we start believing that democracy and liberty for all aren't in the best interests of our country. All it would really take at that point is for one particularly charismatic party leader to argue that in order to protect the opposing party from themselves (and the rest of the country from them as well), we must deprive them of their freedoms and rights, eliminating checks and balances. After all, if opposing partisans are too stupid or corrupt to make good decisions, then we must protect the country from them. Under these conditions, one party will eventually gain enough power to eliminate democracy in favor of a dictatorship.

If you believe "there's no way that could ever happen here," realize that's what most people thought in Germany before Hitler rose to power. Just as Washington predicted, these things can escalate at a shockingly fast rate once the foundation is in place. And before you think that one-party rule doesn't sound so bad, remember that it could be the other party doing the ruling while your party is oppressed.

There is no doubt that we must take action to curb irrational partisanship in this country. But what can we do?

For most of this book, I've discussed things we can do as individuals to alleviate the dangers of irrational partisanship, especially in our individual lives, because the only way to ever fully resolve this problem is if individuals take personal responsibility for doing better. But to focus entirely on personal solutions ignores the systemic environmental factors that contribute to and actively nudge citizens toward irrational partisanship. Many laws affect our perception of the world and our mental health, and government policies affect a variety of social factors that can contribute to mental health problems such as poverty, education, imprisonment, domestic violence, availability of addictive substances, funding for mental health treatments, and so on. In the same way, US political institutions provide the options and incentives that influence voting choices, define political officials' decision-making priorities, and affect the public's expectations of elected officials. For all its strengths, there are some elements of the American political system that foster irrational partisanship in dangerous ways, both among citizens and elected officials. Altering those dangerous components of our political system can play a critical role in de-escalating political tension and thwarting irrational partisanship. If the United States is going to cure partisanship in the long run, voters must insist on institutional reforms in their electoral and political systems.

In this chapter, I'll discuss some potential structural improvements that show strong promise in weakening the salience of partisanship in America. Those reforms are 1) the Alaska voting system, 2) mandatory voting, and 3) an Impartial Party. This list is certainly not exhaustive. I chose these specific reforms because they stand a solid chance at effectively reducing the prevalence and power of irrational partisanship in the United States. Of course, there's no such thing as a perfect system. These suggestions are likely to make things better, not perfect.

The Alaska Voting System

An important driver of irrational partisanship in the United States is the structure of our federal elections. Congressional and presidential elections are subject to winner-take-all rules where the one candidate who gets more votes than any other candidate in a geographic region (state or congressional district) wins the election. That is, regardless of the percentage of voters who actually voted for them, a candidate will win as long as each of the other candidates received fewer votes. For example, if four candidates run for the same seat, the winning candidate could conceivably win with only 26 percent of the vote. In such a scenario, 74 percent of voters would have voted against the winning candidate.

As a result of this setup, only two candidates have a realistic shot at being taken seriously in most US elections because if two Republicans ran for the same senate seat against one Democrat, the Democrat would almost certainly win even in the staunchest Republican county. The system we have virtually dictates that we have only one Republican and one Democrat run for each major political position. And when voters' decisions are limited to only two candidates, they don't need to convince you to vote for them; they simply need to convince you to vote *against* the other candidate. In this system, politicians don't need to be the best candidate for the job; they only need to convince you that the other person is incompetent, dangerous, or evil.

Imagine if this were the case in any other domain of life: for example, if you showed up for a job interview and said, "Look, I'm not the best employee, but the other candidate in the waiting room is an asshole." Any company that used that kind of hiring system would go bankrupt in a very short period of time. If the standard we use to vote for politicians is not acceptable for us in any other area of life, why do we accept it from our political candidates?

Partisans literally cheer this on during political

campaigns and debates. If you listen to any campaign speech, you'll probably notice that the biggest applause lines are attacks on the opponent. Is this really the best way to choose our leaders?

Rather than voting for the best leader, voters often choose the lesser of two evils. For example, in 2016, someone who liked Green Party candidate Jill Stein better than Hillary Clinton was still likely to vote for Clinton because it was the best chance to keep Donald Trump from winning. This political calculus is described by a principle known as Duverger's Law, which suggests that, in winner-take-all elections, the most rational thing to do is vote for the lesser of two evils among the most popular candidates. This is the single most influential factor underlying the seemingly unshakeable duopoly of our current system, where every political question typically offers only two viable competing options. Some other countries operate with different electoral systems that produce more numerous political parties.

Political candidates understand the two-party calculus in the US and go to great lengths to convince their voters that the other party's candidate is evil. Their argument is: "I may not be particularly impressive, but I'm the only thing preventing the other party from ruining your country, life, children, pets, and everything you hold dear. Vote for me, because . . . you have no other choice!"

The lesser-of-two-evils problem directly fuels irrational partisanship. As I've already discussed throughout this book, many partisans rationalize their own party identification by listing everything that's wrong with the opposing party. That is, partisans are increasingly defending their party identification as the lesser of two evils; it's not that they love their party, but that they fear and hate the other party. This increased negativity cultivates allegiance to the only alternative party.[129]

But it doesn't have to be this way—we can change the game. This choice only exists because of the electoral rules we choose. Different electoral rules would change the decision-making process entirely, and Alaska has already done so.

In the 2020 election, the state of Alaska passed a ballot initiative to fundamentally change its election system. Prior to this change, citizens would cast ballots during in-party primary elections to select a candidate for the general election. The candidates they chose would then face off in the general election, and whichever of them received the most votes would be awarded the seat. This is the same plurality system that comprises most election processes throughout the Unites States. The new Alaska system made two important changes that preserve the stability of the current voting system while also improving the extent to which voters' opinions are reflected in official elections.

Under the new Alaska voting system, all candidates appear on the same ballot for the primary election, regardless of their party affiliation. Each voter votes for their preferred candidate, and the top four candidates qualify for the general election. This is known as a jungle primary, and it's nothing new. Other states (including California, Georgia, Louisiana, and Mississippi) have used a similar model. The benefit of having four candidates advance instead of two is that it gives voters more choice in the general election. Importantly, with four candidates in the race instead of two, it makes less sense for a candidate to attack any of the other candidates. This can change the dialogue to focus more on issues, rather than the "good vs. evil" story that is so destructive and counterproductive.

The next part of the Alaska system is just as critical: in the general election, ranked-choice voting is used to determine the winner of the seat. Just as it sounds, ranked-choice voting is a system that allows voters to rank any or all of the four candidates in order of preference. Once all ballots have been cast in the general election, all first-place votes are tallied. If any candidate receives a majority (over 50 percent) of the first-place votes based on this tally, then that candidate wins. But if none of the candidates receive a true majority, then the last-place candidate is eliminated from the race, and all of the votes they received go instead to their voters' second-choice candidate. If this still leaves no majority winner, then the next-lowest-scoring candidate is eliminated as well. This process repeats itself until a single candidate accumulates a majority of the overall vote. The most notable strength of ranked-choice voting is that it completely eliminates the lesser-of-two-evils problem because votes will not be "wasted" on a third-party candidate. Voters can express their real opinion on their first-choice vote while knowing that their most-feared candidate will not benefit from that choice. After all, if my favorite candidate comes in last, then my vote will still count toward my next preferred candidate.

Altogether, the Alaska system plants the seeds for a variety of significant benefits. For one, it provides voters with more options to choose from during general elections. By allowing more candidates to make their case in the lead-up to the general election, voters are given more options to choose from than just the one Democrat or one Republican. Election ballots will likely consist of not only extreme candidates, but also more moderate contenders and perhaps third- or fourth-party nominees.

Currently, many general election debates feature extreme Democrats arguing with extreme Republicans, while reasonable, moderate voices are left completely out of the debate, even though most Americans favor a moderate stance. Additionally, smaller parties often have some very good ideas that address the deepest struggles in our country, but they're rarely heard, because neither of the two-party candidates advocate for that policy. For instance, most Democratic and Republican candidates have opposed marijuana legalization for decades, but a sizable majority of cross-party Americans now favor legalized use. Had we been including minor parties in major political debates, we may have passed legislation on this issue more quickly.

Another advantage of the Alaska system is that it gives elected officials more freedom to disagree with their party without fear of partisan retribution. Currently, elected officials are so afraid of irrational partisans that they see any deviation from the party line as a huge risk. But the Alaska system frees elected officials by making them no longer dependent on irrational partisans' support for their nomination in the primary. That means that under the Alaska system, politicians would actually be incentivized to truly speak their mind and cater to more moderate voters.

Meanwhile, partisan candidates who cater to only the most extreme, angry, and hateful voters in the electorate would be shooting themselves in the foot, as they'd face a greater likelihood of losing the general election to a candidate who speaks to moderates, independents, opposing partisans, and more rational members of both parties.

The Alaska system should also lead to a splintering of the two major parties. It would not dissolve the parties entirely—people would still believe what they believe and find party representatives to express those views—but the parties would become less rigid and dogmatic. This should lead to more successful coalition-building in Congress. By eliminating the lesser-of-two-evils problem, minor parties would have a real chance to win congressional seats. As a result, parties would be more likely to form coalitions by reaching out across party lines and to minor party representatives. In a coalition government, parties actually act in one another's interest. Though they may not always completely agree, they support one another cooperatively, which leads to an overall more effective government. In this scenario, representatives in Congress would be less likely to vote against laws just to make the other party look bad. Overall, this would increase compromise and reduce gridlock in the federal government. Congress would finally start getting things done!

Finally, the Alaska system promotes campaign tactics that are constructive and meaningful, rather than nasty and personal. Candidates who devote their effort to attacking other candidates will find that approach less effective in a ranked-choice voting context. Just because I successfully tear down one candidate doesn't mean voters will then choose me; they might instead go to one of my other opponents.

Furthermore, with ranked-choice voting, candidates

will want to hold favor with voters broadly enough so that they are at least the second- or third-choice on a large number of ballots. When they attack another candidate, they may lose their broader support. In other words, if the prominent Democratic and Republican candidates spend all their time attacking each other, it only increases the chances that a third-party candidate will receive more of the second-place votes, in which case, neither of the top two parties win. Instead, candidates in all parties have an incentive to remain positive in order to attain more of the second- and third-place votes (in addition to their core following's first-place votes).

In short, adopting the Alaska system in your state would double the number of choices you have in the general election while simultaneously disincentivizing fear- and hate-mongering behaviors, instead fostering more constructive and civil political conversation.

Mandatory Voting

Another problem in the United States electoral system is that the electorate does not match the populace. That is, the types of people who vote are predictably different from those who don't vote. Consistent voters tend to be more partisan and ideologically extreme than non-voters or infrequent voters.[130]

According to the Pew Research Center, self-identified partisans—those who say they are either Democrats or Republicans—made up about 57 percent of the population in 2014, but over two-thirds (68 percent) of likely voters in the midterm congressional elections.[131] Extreme partisans make up an even larger segment of the electorate in party primaries, where voters select candidates to run in the general election.[132] As a result, primary candidates pay more attention to partisans and work harder to appeal to them than to moderates. These partisan voters are also less likely than independents and political moderates to support legislative compromise, which means the people most opposed to legislative compromise have a disproportionately large say in which candidates win party primaries.[133]

Consequently, elected officials are reluctant to compromise in office because they are afraid of losing the next primary, where most voters will be extreme partisans.[134] This is one key reason why candidates tend to be so extreme and likely to reject compromise, even when most Americans are moderate and want elected officials to work together to solve problems. It's common to hear people blaming politicians for not compromising, but our current system incentivizes this behavior. If we changed the incentives by changing the system, it's extremely likely we would see much more compromise amongst politicians.

The legislative process requires politicians to be open to compromise, and our country's founders also set our system up in a way that requires collaborative problem-solving; it does not usually allow one side to steamroll the other. Still, irrational partisans punish their elected officials for trying to work with others in such a way. In short, irrational partisans' unwillingness to cooperate prevents effective governance. And the reason they're able to do this is that they're simply more likely to vote consistently.

The solution is not to discourage irrational partisans from participating, or to blunt their voices in any way. It does not serve our country to suppress any of our citizens' voices. Instead, the best solution is to amplify the now-quiet voices of other citizens by increasing voter turnout, and the most direct and effective way to do that is to institute mandatory voting. Quite simply, mandatory voting would mean fining eligible voters who do not show up to voting stations or submit an absentee ballot. To avoid infringing on religious freedoms, people would not be forced to vote, but simply required to show up at the polls on Election Day. States already keep records of eligible voters and track which ones show up at the polls. All that would be required to establish mandatory voting would be for each state to mail out a small fine to any eligible voters who did not show up at any point during the election. Of course, mandatory voting would be less burdensome if it were accompanied by other reforms that make voting easier, such as expanding early voting, providing paid time off, or making Election Day a national holiday.

Mandatory voting is not unprecedented, as at least eighteen other countries—including Australia, Belgium, Egypt, Mexico, and Turkey—currently require eligible voters to show up to the polls, even if they do not cast a ballot.[135] Based on the outcomes we see in other countries, mandatory voting is very likely to increase the percentage of eligible voters who show up to the polls. For example, Australia enacted mandatory voting in 1924, and voter turnout jumped from roughly 60 percent prior to the law, to over 90 percent in the 1925 election. Belgium also practices mandatory voting and boasts the highest turnout of any nation (87 percent), compared to only 55 percent in the United States.[136] Mandatory voting would make American election results more representative of the will of the people.

The primary benefit of mandatory voting is that it would reduce the disproportional partisan influence over elections and the dangerous polarization that stems from that control. Because mandatory voting would primarily raise the number of moderates and independents who vote, and because those types of voters tend to look favorably on legislative compromise, elected officials would have more incentive to reach across party lines and work together.[137] This kind of behavior reduces congressional gridlock and makes governments function more effectively. Mandatory voting is also likely to influence candidates' campaign strategies.

Right now, candidates tend to devote most of their resources to getting their partisan base to the polls—that is, Republican candidates try to get fellow Republicans to vote, while the Democratic candidates focus on getting Democrats to the voting booths. In order to mobilize their partisan voters, and because fear is such a strong motivator, elected officials often spend the bulk of their effort on negative attacks and divisive issues. As a result, partisans end up casting their votes out of fear of the opposing candidate, rather than enthusiasm for their own. If candidates don't have to deploy costly get-out-the-vote campaigns, they could either spend less time raising money (and more time serving their constituents), or they could direct those funds to other constructive efforts.

In addition to a fine for not voting, there's also the option to offer all voters a chance to win a voter lottery. This interesting suggestion came from Thomas Mann and Norman Ornstein.[138] In this solution, everyone who votes would be assigned a number, and a drawing would be held soon after Election Day. Hypothetically, the federal government could give something like $1,000,000 to one voter and $50,000 to another twenty voters just by reallocating the money we currently spend on get-out-the-vote initiatives to the lottery.

If people are willing to wait in line at a gas station for a lottery ticket that gives them a one-in-300 million chance of winning, they're probably willing to wait in line for the chance to win $1,000,000. In fact, their odds of winning would be better than those of winning the actual lottery, plus there would be a guaranteed winner! A voter lottery could also reward those who consistently vote by awarding them with more tickets, say if people received one ticket for each consecutive election for which they've shown up. Provide non-voters both a carrot in the form of lottery tickets and a stick that costs them money if they don't show up to vote. See how this changes voting patterns.

Unfortunately, any reform to the political system will certainly be blocked if either party believes it will benefit their opponents. If there is one thing we've learned in this book, it's that partisans don't think according to principles or values, but in terms of what will get their party a victory on election day. You can make all the logical and evidentiary arguments you want in favor of an electoral reform, but it has no chance if one party believes it will harm their status. We have already seen this play out in efforts to promote vote-by-mail or to allow people convicted of a felony to vote. Republican partisans (mistakenly) got it into their head that those reforms would benefit Democrats, so they categorically oppose both reforms exclusively on that party-line argument.

In today's politics, justice, fairness, logic, and facts don't matter; all that matters is which party will benefit, because the only thing that partisans care about is keeping the other party from gaining any power. Should Puerto Rico and Washington D.C. become states? There are very good arguments both for and against statehood. None of them matter, though, nor does it matter whether it's "fair" to provide representation in the Senate for legal US citizens in these regions. All that matters to the debate is that both new states would likely elect Democrats to Congress, and for that reason alone, Democrats support statehood and Republicans oppose it. The arguments are pointless because partisans are more focused on protecting themselves than doing what's best for the country. For partisans, "If it benefits my party, it's good; if it benefits the other party, it's bad."

Although Republican partisans push the idea that any effort to boost turnout would undoubtedly benefit Democrats, the actual evidence suggests that neither party would gain an advantage from mandatory voting. In fact, an interesting study suggests that, if anything, mandatory voting may give a slight edge to Republicans over Democrats.

According to Colin Woodard from Politico:

"Nonvoters as a whole are fairly reflective of the broader electorate in terms of political preferences. If they were to all vote in November, 33 percent say they would support Democrats; 30 percent, Republicans; and 18 percent, a third-party candidate. More surprisingly perhaps, and potentially more consequential for November, these numbers gently tilt in the opposite direction in many battleground states, with nonvoters choosing Trump over the as-yet-undetermined Democratic nominee 36 to 28 percent in Pennsylvania, 34 to 25 percent in Arizona, and 30 to 29 percent in New Hampshire. Wisconsin and Michigan mirror the national average, favoring the Democrat 33 to 31 percent and 32 to 31 percent, respectively, while in Georgia the margin is 34 to 29 percent. This data challenges many long-standing assumptions of political experts."[139]

Of course, these results are specific to the 2020 election, and were taken at a time when the Democratic nominee was not yet determined. Nevertheless, they do indicate that increasing turnout would bring in a roughly equal portion of Democrats and Republicans.

Increasing voter turnout should not be a partisan issue, but it has become one because of misunderstandings about the types of people who do not vote. Again, neither party would gain an electoral advantage from mandatory voting, or from any other efforts to increase turnout. No one has anything to fear from efforts to get more people to vote, because those efforts would bring in a roughly equal share of both Republican and Democratic voters. What's more, recent efforts by Republican state legislatures to make it more difficult to vote are likely to decrease turnout among both Democrats and Republicans.

The Impartial Party

As George Washington warned us in his farewell address, political parties breed perverse and undemocratic incentives for their members. The current political system rewards politicians for Party loyalty over country loyalty and punishes elected officials for openly criticizing their party leaders, which is the antithesis of a free and open marketplace of ideas. Most destructive of all, our current electoral system creates a game where winning matters above all else—even above our nation's ability to function. The two-party duopoly that we currently embrace discourages the healthy, productive, and pro-democratic values our country was founded on. Adding more parties to the American political conversation will not cure what ails us if those parties are all motivated by self-gratifying, undemocratic principles. The solution to irrational partisanship is not multiplying two irrational parties into many more.

What we need is a political party that puts the good of the nation above the good of the party. To this end, I propose an Impartial Party to compete with the two major political parties. Unlike other so-called "Independent" parties, the Impartial Party will not have an established platform or prescribed policies that candidates and members must adopt. Anyone can join and be free to believe whatever they want. The only requirement for membership is a desire to disrupt the two-party duopoly that currently dominates American politics. The Impartial Party fosters dissent, disagreement, independence, pragmatism, and collaborative compromise. The Impartial Party rejects tribalism and political obedience in all forms, and instead values national health over any political party, including the Impartial Party!

What we need most is a political party that is truly impartial—a party that does not demand loyalty to any Party, organization, special interest, or ideology. Members of the Impartial Party only require loyalty to your own individual political principles. These Impartials will vote with their conscience and not take any responsibility for other members of their party.

The Impartial Party will hold very few uncompromising issue stances. Instead, they will value only open and constructive disagreements, and free and tolerant (i.e., humble) expressions of views. Leaders of the Impartial Party will care less about winning the next election than about having individual pride in the personal actions they've taken in office. No one will be punished (officially or reputationally) by the party for expressing an opinion contrary to anyone else's—so long as the opinion is purposefully developed and well-thought-out.

Impartials will celebrate disagreement and, as such, look for opportunities to facilitate open dialogue while opposing any effort to silence political opponents. Because their specific actions are not based on any theoretical party positions, but rather on thoughtful dialogue about the specific issue, Impartials would promote extensive legislative amendments so we could constantly update or tweak policies as we see their real-world consequences unfold over time. Most of all, Impartials will fully and completely trust citizens to make rational and informed voting decisions, even if everyone doesn't ultimately agree with one another on the specifics. The Impartial party opposes any policy that's meant to disenfranchise voters. Finally, rather than attacking the other candidates or parties, Impartials will focus on what they want to do to make America, and the world, a better place.

Our country's current electoral process has created a duopoly where only two parties have room to vie for our attention and support. Because humans are more motivated by fear than any positive incentive, these two politicians (the successful ones, at least) devote the bulk of their effort to tearing each other down in order to scare us into action. And those of us who are unwilling to cave to their fear tactics are left to choose between the lesser of two evils.

To get to the root of this problem, I propose three specific systemic improvements: 1) the Alaska voting system—to generate more options for voters and disincentivize negative campaigning; 2) mandatory voting—to make our elections more representative of the entire country and disincentivize candidates from catering to extreme partisans; and 3) establishment of the Impartial Party, which would prioritize the country's health above all else, rejecting political correctness and dogma in favor of individual engagement expression, as well as collaborative problem-solving.

Treatment: Fight to Save Democracy

Unlike in previous chapters, I'm not going to ask you to write in your journal or talk to your friends and family. No, this step in the process calls for something bigger and more earth-shattering . . . OK, maybe that's a little much.

This is the point in the book where we move from inward improvement to trying to improve our surroundings. Of course, you are free to do whatever you want, but I hope you will take some time to advocate for whatever governmental reforms you believe will have a positive outcome for America and the entire human race.

If you support any of the policies I described above, I hope you will advocate for them with friends and family, but also to your elected representatives. A political movement doesn't happen on its own; it requires the hard work and persistence of millions of people striving for a common goal. To be clear, I do not want you to advocate any policy that you oppose, or even find questionable. Rather, I ask that you promote policies that you strongly believe would make the world a better place.

Too many of us believe that supporting the "right" party is enough to create change, but that is simply naïve. In American politics, those who fight for what they believe in are much more likely to get what they want. It also helps if you have billions of dollars, but there isn't much we can do about that.

If you support any policy that will improve society, I hope you will contact your state legislators, governor, congressperson, senator, and even president. It's easier than you think. If you visit www.commoncause.org/find-your-representative/, you'll find a list of your representatives, their phone numbers, mailing addresses, and email addresses. Just send them an email or fill out a contact form on their webpages. They want to hear from their constituents, so let's all tell them that we want a government that functions more effectively, doesn't discriminate against opposing partisans, and most of all does not force us to choose between the lessor of two evils. If there is a policy you believe would reduce irrational partisanship that I haven't mentioned, tell your representatives that you want it.

Below are links to organizations devoted to improving American democracy and reducing partisanship. If you want to weaken the two-party duopoly, you'll probably find at least some of the policies promoted by these groups to your liking. I don't agree with 100 percent of what these organizations advocate, but they provide some valuable ways to organize action that can bring about governmental reforms.

- National Association of Nonpartisan Reformers: nonpartisanreformers.org
- Fairvote: www.fairvote.org
- Bipartisan Policy Center: bipartisanpolicy.org
- New America: www.newamerica.org

CHAPTER 11

How to Talk about Politics

"The partisan, when he is engaged in a dispute, cares nothing about the rights of the question, but is anxious only to convince his hearers of his own assertions."

—Plato

As a professor of American politics, part of my job is to facilitate informative and enriching discussions about occasionally controversial topics. During my classes, students debate some emotionally-laden issues, such as affirmative action, the death penalty, gun control, immigration, and marijuana legalization. (OK, maybe that last one isn't so controversial in a room full of college students.) These lively discussions are held both in-person and virtually, but regardless of the setting, they hardly ever become heated, personal, angry, or nasty. Of course, it helps that I'm there to dissuade any student from getting heated during our discussions. Nevertheless, my students actually seem to enjoy expressing their opinions and hearing opposing perspectives. Personally, these discussions give me hope that Americans can indeed engage in pleasant and enlightening dialogue about politics—when they know how to manage such conversations effectively.

Unfortunately, typical political discussions in America are not nearly as warm and fuzzy outside of my classroom.

The open, inquisitive, and friendly environment of the classroom stands in stark contrast to what I see in real life and on the internet. In face-to-face interactions, people usually avoid any mention of politics unless they're completely positive that everyone within earshot agrees with what they have to say. And while this behavior is obviously dysfunctional, I'll take it over the feces-hurling that poses for political discussion on the internet any day.

The cloak of online anonymity frees people to release the most monstrous versions of their inner nastiness, arrogance, and irrationality. When I peruse discussion boards, whether on political or non-political websites, I rarely come across anything that resembles friendly or productive discussion. That's a shame, because the internet gives us the ability to learn from people all over the world, yet too many use it as an opportunity to yell at one another.

It seems that most Americans share my gloomy view of political discussion. In a 2019 Pew Research poll, 85 percent of Americans said that "Over the last several years, the tone and nature of political debate in this country has become more negative." Moreover, most people say political debate has become less: respectful (85 percent), fact-based (76 percent), and issue-focused (60 percent). In the same poll, half of Americans said that talking about politics with people they disagree with is "generally stressful and frustrating."[140]

Being afraid of open political discussion does nothing to help Americans or the country as a whole. In fact, there's compelling evidence that people benefit from political discussion. Talking about politics spreads awareness and understanding. It also and raises the quality of our ideas and opinions on challenging issues, and there's evidence that political discussion makes us more likely to participate in the political system.[141] Furthermore, talking with people who hold different opinions makes us sharper in our thinking and better able to articulate our views, while helping us to better understand the reasons behind different perspectives.[142] Most relevant to this book, when we understand the deepest value-based motivations behind opposing perspectives, it increases our humility and tolerance toward people who hold opposing opinions.[143]

Although political discussion can be incredibly beneficial, the benefits depend a great deal on how we engage in political discourse. Political discussion is most valuable when it involves diverse and contradictory perspectives, which are shared non-defensively in a civil manner. Unfortunately, our society is more likely to hold political discussions in groups where everyone already agrees with one another.[144] Liberals usually talk about politics with other liberals, while conservatives mostly talk with other conservatives. But for political discussion to be enlightening, it needs to include people who hold dissimilar political viewpoints.

Conversations that involve Democrats and Republicans, liberals and conservatives tend to increase humility, understanding, and tolerance. This arrangement helps us see the reasonable motivations, desires, and insights that opposing partisans bring to the table.[145] These productive discussions can also challenge stereotypes. As we discussed in Chapter 5, we're likely to see opposing partisans as more extreme than they really are, but when we actually talk with them, we learn that those stereotypes are mostly exaggerated hogwash.

This brings us to the other half of the equation: in order to be enlightening, political discussions must take place in a calm, disinterested, civil manner. Research shows that most people are turned off by uncivil discussions about politics.[146] Indeed, uncivil discussions heat up negative feelings, which only makes us more closed-minded as we see greater fundamental disagreement with the opposing side.[147] In contrast, when a discussion is more detached and curious, we're more likely to gain a new understanding of opposing arguments, more respect and tolerance for the opposition, and increased trust in the government.[148] In other words, you're only likely to benefit from political discussion when it is civil.

Choosing civility when you're discussing politics with opposing partisans can actually help cure *their* irrational partisanship. Recall from Chapter 5 that one of the primary contributors to irrational partisanship is an exaggerated fear of the other party. Our fear of opposing partisans comes from inaccurate perceptions of who they are and the beliefs they hold. Irrational partisans assume that members of the opposing party are ignorant, extreme, and immoral. These perceptions lead to limited contact with opposing partisans and misunderstandings about the motivations that underlie their political views. But when we communicate openly and non-defensively with members of the opposing party, we're more likely to identify the similarities we share with them. In social psychology, this is a concept known as the contact hypothesis, and it's been shown to increase tolerance and lower hostility.

Humble and friendly interaction with opposing partisans helps us to replace overgeneralized stereotypes with more accurate perceptions of their human goals, values, dreams, and interests so we can better understand why they hold opinions that are different from ours. This reduces our fear, hostility, and anger. Having close contact with people of different political views shows us that while we may not agree on everything, we're a lot alike in many of the most important ways. Where echo chambers focus our attention on exaggerated differences, one-on-one friendly contact opens our world and gives us new insight.

The purpose of this chapter is to provide specific guidelines to help you engage in civil and productive discussions of political issues. These guidelines are based on previous research and my experiences leading political discussions in the classroom. Each one can help minimize the anger and hostilities that often accompany political debates. I should point out that this list does not include obvious standards of appropriate behavior for discussions (such as not interrupting others or engaging in childish name-calling). Instead, what follows is a list of simple ways to make ordinary political discussions more fruitful and less emotionally toxic.

Establish Your Goals

What do you want to get out of a political discussion? If you're like me, your goal is to understand the perspectives of other people. From a selfish standpoint, you'll get more out of any debate by listening and learning from others than you would simply waiting for your turn to speak. After all, you already know what your opinion is and why you hold it, so it doesn't benefit you to elaborate for everyone else on all the reasons why you're right. Instead, you'll gain much more knowledge about the world and other people by listening and working to understand their perspectives.

Please don't get me wrong—by all means, talk! Pose clarifying questions or ask for their view on a hypothetical situation to learn the nuances of their perspective. State your opinion while keeping an open mind. But your goal for every debate should be to understand someone else's perspective and to work toward a practical solution.

Contrarily, if your goal is to persuade others, you'll likely wind up disappointed. I'm not saying it's wrong to persuade others to your side; indeed, much of the national political discourse is about trying to persuade people. But the problem arises when we tie our own satisfaction with the conversation to our ability (or inability) to persuade others to our side. It's fine to try to persuade, but if you make that your highest goal in a conversation, you will quickly become frustrated—and so will everyone else. And if your primary aim is to persuade others, you'll often end up resenting people when they fail to conform to your perspective. This is a very unhealthy, and ultimately counterproductive, way to live your life. You must accept that people are free to hold whatever position they choose.

More than anything, do not blame others when they fail to "see the correctness" of your views. A healthier response is to accept that some people are not going to be persuaded, no matter how good you think your arguments are or how many facts you throw out. What you could do is take responsibility for your inability to persuade others. Rather than blaming others for their stupidity, it's better to acknowledge that maybe your understanding of their perspective is less accurate than you thought it was, and because of that, your arguments were not persuasive enough. After all, if people were not persuaded, then your arguments (by definition) were unpersuasive. That doesn't necessarily mean your arguments couldn't persuade other people in other contexts, but they were unpersuasive here.

Placing the weakness (and opportunity for improvement) on your side of the interaction can motivate you to develop better arguments, seek a deeper understanding, or simply accept that people are different and will respond differently to the same statements. All of these reactions are healthier than becoming heated and angry with everyone who fails to recognize the brilliance and ultimate authority of your political views, and these strategies will also promote better interpersonal relationships.

When discussing politics with irrational partisans, it's especially important to remember that they have a mental illness. Have you ever tried to convince a smoker, alcoholic, or drug addict that their addiction is bad for them, and that they should stop? This is not an effective approach to get them to quit. In fact, it's likely they'll become even more irrational, defensive, and angry. But don't you expect that to some extent? Do you really expect a smoker to stop when you tell them "those things will kill you"?

When you're dealing with someone you know has a mental illness, it makes no sense to become angry and frustrated with them. Their mind is not working properly, and they are highly unlikely to respond in ways a rational person would expect. Treat them as someone you are trying to help—not by calling them wrong or irrational, but by listening to them and helping them hear the reasons for your opinion. In fact, the best way to change their mind about your opinion is to explain why you believe what you do in a non-combative and non-defensive way. They probably won't change their entire opinion, but they will likely recognize the validity of your concerns, and your views will be more likely to resonate with them.

Approach them with kindness and acceptance, and they'll be more likely to respond to you in kind.

Don't Take It Personally

Another piece of advice I'd offer you is to disconnect your sense of personal identity from your opinions and beliefs about the world. In my experience, the main reason disagreement causes anger is that people take their political opinions personally. That is, they believe their opinions so adamantly that those opinions have become essential to their identity, so when someone else accepts or rejects that belief, it feels like they're accepting or rejecting them as a person.

Unfortunately, pride gets in the way of productive political discussions because we grow angry and defensive when our opinions are challenged. When we encounter political arguments that challenge our identity-level beliefs, we experience cognitive dissonance and an intensely negative emotional state.[149] Additionally, people today tend to believe that if their opinion is possibly incorrect, then they must not have the fundamental capacity for intelligence or critical thinking. And when they feel the pressure of a particular view being challenged, it can lower their self-esteem. If exposure to opposing arguments threatens our self-esteem, it should come as no surprise that we dislike and avoid those who contradict and challenge our opinions!

While thinking less of yourself when you "lose" a political argument is perfectly understandable, you don't have to live as a slave to that feeling. You can give it a moment to pass, and then make a new choice. Imagine for a second that you hold an incomplete or even incorrect view or idea. If someone comes along and helps you correct or improve your understanding of the situation, you are now smarter than you were before. In fact, you might even feel better about yourself after losing an argument, because you learned. You overcame your pride, and now you're better and smarter for it. The problem is that some people are so afraid of looking stupid that they would rather "win" and be wrong than "lose" and learn something new.

The irony is that when we defensively avoid admitting any lack of knowledge, we ultimately end up more stupid and incompetent than we would have been if we had simply opened ourselves up with a little humility.

Another approach to this self-esteem problem is to recognize that human value is incredibly multifaceted. There are many different ways you can bring value to others, so to judge your entire self-worth on a single characteristic or shortcoming minimizes what you bring to the world in an extreme way. And who's to say what that one most important value is, anyway? As I explained in Chapter 8, there's no universal way to rank the various strengths that people bring to the world, and what one person views as a generally positive trait, another might view as generally negative.

While it's true that competence and topical

intelligence are important, other factors such as adaptability, experimentation, and humility are also important. Returning to our original discussion, let's consider a situation where you (rightly) lose an argument and then begin to think differently about the topic you were debating. In this case, you could choose to see yourself as either unintelligent or growth-oriented. Some may see you as open-minded and mature, while others may see you as stupid or worthless—but how someone else sees you tells us more about them than it does about you.

Regardless, it doesn't do any good to think about how someone else perceives you. Instead, try to focus on what you're hearing and learning in the conversation. After all, if someone were to stop being your friend because you couldn't make a strong political argument, were they really a worthwhile friend to begin with?

Focus on Values Over Facts

When you're talking about politics, it's almost always best to focus on values rather than facts and evidence. I know that sounds backwards, but hear me out: if you find yourself writing a research paper or addressing the technical aspects of a political question, then you should certainly base your assertions on scientific data as much as possible. During most political conversations, however, the discussion doesn't ultimately come down to technical specifications. The debate is really over how to weigh competing values in a certain scenario. The best approach you can take is to explain your political position by linking it back to the relevant values that underlie it.

Earlier in the book, I explained the five common values—Security, Opportunity, Freedom, Fairness, and Tranquility—that sit beneath most political issues. When you're having a political conversation, consider which of these values is motivating your opinion, then explain why that value matters to you and why you think it may be worth making the necessary sacrifices in this situation to attain it. When you emphasize the values that uphold your beliefs, it helps others empathize and engage with you less defensively. Most likely, you both have similar concerns, goals, and interests, though you may balance them differently in specific scenarios. Focusing your attention on these commonalities shows opposing partisans that you are a reasonable person who happens to hold a different perspective. Although they may not change their mind, they are more likely to respect your stance while feeling less hostility against you.

Facts are secondary to the values at play in political discussions. It's easy to ignore facts, and some might simply consider them evidence of your bias and brainwashing. When you try to base your arguments on facts without discussing values, others can simply dismiss your statements as politically motivated. And if they've reached the point where they're saying, "I don't believe that for a second," you really have no recourse but to drop the subject. Otherwise, you enter into a completely different and unproductive discussion, where you must defend the accuracy and objectivity of your information source. It doesn't mean they're necessarily right, but it kills the conversation when you try to defend yourself.

Politicians shamelessly use this tactic whenever they encounter news they don't like. Just call the news source "biased" or "fake news," and their partisan followers have an excuse to completely ignore whatever evidence makes them look bad. Of course, this is also the same approach cult leaders use to ensure they are the only voice of authority for their followers. Everyone who disputes what the leader says is labeled a non-believer, and must be wrong for that reason alone. But when you explain your views in terms of your values, the opposing party cult members won't be able to so easily dismiss your arguments.

Ignore Motivations

Once, I was sitting with a friend at a bar (where intelligent discussions often happen), and we saw a commercial encouraging people to buckle their seat belts. It turns out that he and I disagreed on whether such seat belt commercials were a worthwhile investment. I opposed them because they don't seem to work, but my friend saw it differently. At one point in our conversation, I innocently asked him, "Have you seen any evidence that seat belt ad campaigns work?" To my surprise, this made him upset, and instead of using my question to carry the conversation forward, he responded with, "Do you have any evidence they don't work?!"

The miscommunication was over our motivations. I just wanted to find the right answer. I genuinely wanted to know if there was any research showing that seat belt ad campaigns were effective, but he interpreted my questions as a rhetorical attempt to win the argument. He was right of course, that absence of evidence is not evidence of absence, but I wasn't trying to corner him with his lack of evidence.

The point I'm trying to make here is that, sometimes, other people sincerely do want to get to the bottom of the truth. A more productive response from my friend would have been, "I'm not aware of any, but then I haven't really looked either." Then again, I also could have been more sensitive to the phrasing of my own question, and instead said, "I wonder if there is any evidence on this. Have you seen any research on the topic?" This would have made my intent more clear, and also made it much easier for him to say no in response.

When our goal during political discussion is to "win," we presume that everyone else has the same motivation. This presumption of competitiveness alters how we interpret otherwise innocent questions and statements. Instead, when you make it your goal to unearth the truth, and when you take the position of a free agent instead of preemptively taking a side, you will find political discussions to be much more friendly, polite, and informative.

When it comes to political arguments, it's also important to avoid turning your rebuffs into personal attacks. This might sound obvious, but I have found that people don't often realize when they're doing this. As a general rule, it is best to attack specific arguments and ignore the personal characteristics of the arguer entirely. The quality of an argument has nothing to do with the person making the argument, unless they are basing it on their own credibility. For example, if the dumbest person alive believes that the earth is round, does that mean the earth must be flat? Of course not, but that often seems like a compelling argument to make when your back is against the wall and you're trying to defend your opinions and beliefs.

When you respond to an argument with remarks about the person who's making the argument, it's called an "ad hominem attack." For example, imagine I argued that state governments should increase their funding for higher education because it would improve the economy, but you respond with, "Of course you would say that—you're a college professor and would benefit from increased funding." It may well be the case that I benefit from increased higher education funding, but that is irrelevant to my claim that it would benefit the economy. Is it not possible that I would benefit from more funding, *and* it would also improve the economy? If I'm wrong, I'm wrong. Prove it—not by tearing me down or questioning my motives, but by addressing the specific issue.

Argue against the arguments, not the arguer. Try to work collaboratively with the other person to better understand the situation and each other.

Assume People Are Smart

One of my best friends thinks I'm a complete idiot. All right, that's a little extreme, but he definitely knows that he's smarter than me. This friend has a very authoritarian way of looking at intelligence. In brief, he only listens to people whom he believes are smarter than him and completely ignores what the "dumb" people have to say. He's like the stereotypical uncle or grandfather who thinks he's always right.

During one of our discussions, we got on the topic of political psychology, a subject I happen to be well informed on. While my friend had only a passing interest in the topic, I had spent over a decade studying it, and even published journal articles on the topic. None of that mattered! In his mind, he was smarter than I, and for this reason alone, all my thoughts were irrelevant and not even worth the time to consider. As he saw it, his job was to explain the truth to the less intelligent. The fact that I disagreed with him was just evidence of my ignorance. Ultimately, he refused to learn anything from me and continued to labor under a misunderstanding of the current research. If only he had considered the possibility that I might have something to offer to the conversation, he would have learned something new from our conversation (without the need to ultimately change his opinion).

The lesson here is that it's best to assume that other people have something of value to say, whether they have decades of experience or none at all. Sometimes, you may need to dig through some frustrating comments to get to their insight. And sometimes, you might need to dig through poor verbal skills that don't quite express what they really mean. But what do you lose in such a situation? All it requires is that you politely listen to another human being for a few minutes. And very often, when you bring this attitude, you'll find that the other person actually has some perspective you haven't considered, or life experiences you haven't had.

It is far better to assume that whomever you're talking to is actually smart in some way and knows something you don't. By assuming that others are smart (even if they don't always act that way), you're more likely to actually listen to what they have to say. Treating people like they're smart and have something valuable to offer also makes you a more likable, popular human being. Have you ever had someone talk to you like you're an idiot? It doesn't feel very good. I once worked with someone who talked to everyone as if we were all five years old. At first, I absolutely hated interacting with him and avoided his presence at all costs. Eventually, though, I realized he deserved pity rather than contempt. His attitude made it nearly impossible for him to connect closely with others or to learn anything from them—which he surely felt, even if he didn't know how to handle it better. His condescending communication style damaged his relationships with other people.

During political discussions, the big mistake you want to avoid is assuming that people are uninformed simply because they express an opposing point of view. As we saw in the previous chapters, just because someone disagrees with you does not mean they are stupid or biased; maybe they have information that you are not aware of, or a different perspective that you have never considered before. Maybe they can help clarify your own opinions or even change your mind altogether. You will never know unless you really listen and consider what they have to say. If you enter into a discussion assuming that you know everything, then political discourse truly is a waste of your time. Give people the benefit of the doubt, and you may be surprised by how much they can teach you.

Accept That You Could Be Wrong

On a related note, it's usually best to hold both your personal opinions and even your evidence-based beliefs with humility. Too often, we can feel certain that our way of interpreting the world is the correct and complete view of things. This is largely thanks to the Dunning-Kruger effect, which is when we see ourselves as having expertise on things we really have little to no real experience in. In political discussions, this means we overestimate our understanding of a topic precisely because we are unaware of how much information we lack.

When we have low levels of information on a topic, we often believe that we do know all of the relevant details, which makes us overconfident in our view and less likely to listen to others. If you think you know a lot about political issues just because you've watched the news or thought about it a little bit, chances are you're falling under the spell of the Dunning-Kruger effect.

Furthermore, being overconfident in the correctness of your opinions might even make you angry toward anyone who expresses an opposing argument. If I believe that I know all there is to know about a topic, and you come to a different conclusion than mine, it must be because you lack information or intelligence. This overconfident sense of certainty makes us more likely to engage in a competitive style of argument where we see discussion as a win-or-lose sport, rather than a positive-sum exchange of ideas.[150] Treating discussions like competitions where victory is necessary is exactly what leads to hurt feelings, hostility, and frayed relationships.

Listen

This brings me to my final piece of advice, which is to actually listen to what other people have to say. In any discussion (not just political ones), listening is the most valuable skill. Too often, we can be so eager to explain our point that we fail to really hear and consider what the other person is saying. When other people are talking, try putting yourself in their shoes to get a sense of their true reasoning and perspective. After all, you cannot really understand your own opinion without understanding the opposing views.

In *On Liberty*, John Stuart Mill put it well when he stated, "He who knows only his own side of the case knows little of that. His reasons may be good, and no one may have been able to refute them. But if he is equally unable to refute the reasons on the opposite side, if he does not so much as know what they are, he has no ground for preferring either opinion."[151]

Believing that you are right and that you have strong evidence for your position does not justify ignoring the arguments of other people, yet that is often the reason for our unproductive and inefficient political discussions. You have far more to gain from learning the viewpoints of others than you do by asserting and re-asserting the arguments you already know. Of course, I'm not saying you should never express your views; if everyone only listened, there would be no discussion! Instead, when you're not talking, it's important that you actually listen to other people and try to understand where they're coming from. Doing so will allow you to better respond to what they say, and also make them feel like you actually respect their point of view, which then builds the environment for a real exchange of ideas so you can both learn and start getting things done.

A Better Approach

When you do talk about politics with others, it's important

to take the right approach. Far too many people avoid discussing politics because they are afraid of angering someone or creating an unnecessary problem in the relationship. It doesn't have to be this way. We can make it much easier to talk about politics in a civil and polite manner. In fact, there are only two things you have to do to have a dispassionate discussion of politics:

First, spend time actually listening to what other people say instead of waiting for your turn to speak. People can tell when you're not listening, and they don't like having their concerns ignored. Neither would you! When you're listening, try to identify exactly why they believe their point of view is the correct one. What deep concerns underlie it? Look at the discussion as an opportunity to learn from others, rather than a chance to show them why you're right and they're wrong.

Second, when it is your chance to talk, simply explain the values behind your opinion. Resist the urge to challenge and dispute anything they say. Believe me, I know this can be difficult—students will often say some pretty idiotic things during class discussion, some of which are factually incorrect, but I bite my tongue and don't correct what they say (unless of course it relates to course material). Disputing what someone says makes them defensive, which triggers motivated reasoning (see Chapter 6) and adds to their anger. Defensiveness is a common reaction, so it's usually best to let it slide. Instead, focus only on explaining your reasons for your beliefs. If you can relate your political beliefs to your life experiences, social situation, or personality, even better. This is what is most effective in helping others understand where you're coming from.

Irrational partisanship and extreme political hostility may seem like intractable problems, but they're really not. Political differences can certainly be difficult to face and will always cause at least occasional frustration, but that tension is actually an indicator of a healthy, open, and collaborative society. Irrational partisanship, on the other hand, is a pathology, and we all have a hand in healing it.

By taking ownership for your personal attitude toward politics, toward others, and toward your conversations, you can initiate a grassroots-level shift that produces ripple effects and creates a better society for all of us. By calling for small adjustments in the electoral process, you can set up a different set of rules to prevent this kind of escalation from happening again. By holding your political elites and media spokespeople to higher and more accurate standards, you can change the environment for political discourse. And by practicing humility and listening more intently, you can begin to mend the damage that's been done and start to find some collaborative solutions moving forward.

After all, hating someone solely for their political beliefs is like despising people who cover their hamburgers with mayonnaise.

Conclusion

Throughout this book, I've made my case for why irrational partisanship is a mental illness and should be treated as such. I've offered you tools to help you become more aware of your own biases, tips for dealing with the irrational partisans in your own life, and resources to help you get more accurate and less manipulated information. I've even offered you some guidance on how you can take action to change our electoral system, which is one of the key issues at the root of irrational partisanship. But perhaps some of the most important work you can do to start curing partisanship now is talking to your neighbors, friends, and colleagues—but not about politics . . . yet.

One of the best ways to reduce political hostility in this country is for Democrats and Republicans to engage more with one another non-politically. That's right, I'm suggesting that when you initially meet members of the opposing party, you first talk about things that have nothing to do with politics. When you're talking to someone who disagrees with you about politics, try bringing up challenges and goals you may have in common. You might talk about your careers, children, sports, gardening, pets, community, or anything else. It's fine to discuss politics later on, once you've built some rapport and established a foundation of common humanity. But beginning with your common ground shows both of you that you're not that different from one another. It sets the stage for more productive political conversation, and more than that, it strengthens the fabric of daily civil life.

For example, when I am at my child's soccer game, I have no idea what political party the other parents belong to, and I don't care in the slightest. We're all parents who face similar parenting and home-life challenges, and we all want the best for our children. We cheer on and high-five each other's kids when they score a goal or play good defense.

There's a good chance one of your close relationships has already suffered under the influence of partisanship, so don't let it take more from you. The more you focus on shared interests, circumstances, and goals, the less partisanship will interfere with or destroy your social connections. Remember, partisanship is just one expression of who a person is, and not a very comprehensive one at that.

One other way to build a better foundation for cross-party relationships is through an intentional process called vicarious contact. In social psychology, the contact hypothesis states that contact with members of opposing political groups reduces prejudice and makes us more tolerant. Interestingly, though, this contact doesn't have to be in-person. Instead, vicarious contact with people from dissimilar political groups can have just as much of an effect as face-to-face contact.

What exactly is vicarious contact? It can simply be exposure to opposing partisans and their lives on television or other media (note that this excludes irrational partisan media). Watching shows where real people express themselves or reading opinion columns from opposing partisans can both have this positive effect. Usually, opinion columns lay out strong arguments regarding political policies. These articles are unlikely to change your mind on a particular issue, but they can help you understand why the other party is doing what they're doing, and often reveal that they have good reasons behind their stance on a policy.

Once you feel you are ready, start engaging your friends and relatives in political discussions. It won't always be easy, and you'll certainly find times where discussions are frustrating and unproductive. Hell, that happens to me too, and I wrote a damn book about how to stop it! Of course, if other people are unwilling or incapable of engaging in productive discussions, you need to know when to move on and talk about something else. If you can't engage in a productive conversation where each of you take turns listening and explaining your value-based opinions, sometimes it's best to just let it go.

So, the time has come to take what you've learned in this book and start using it in the real world. Once you understand the non-political things you have in common, engage in political discussions with your friends and family. Accept that you could be wrong and that your self-worth has nothing to do with which political party you support. Start watching mainstream news instead of getting your hour of hate from partisan media. Fight for real change in the political system by destroying the two-party establishment before it makes us destroy each other.

And if you're interested in continuing the discussion about irrational partisanship and how to stop it, I invite you to visit my website, www.disagreeingagreeably.com, so we can keep learning together. If you would like to engage in political discussions with members of the other Party, there are online resources that can help. The websites below will pair you up with people from the opposing party and has you engage in guided discussions about politics that will help you understand why people holding opposing opinions.

Braver Angels:
https://braverangels.org/

Living Room Conversations:
https://livingroomconversations.org/

American Public Square:
https://americanpublicsquare.org/

ACKNOWLEDGMENTS

This book is dedicated to anyone who has ever had a political conversation with me. Too many people had to endure my insufferable argumentation, ignorance, and arrogance. It is only because of them that I learned what *not* to do during political discussions. Of course, this book would never have happened without Jackson Gray Smith providing me the daily inspiration to make the world a better place. Furthermore, I want to thank Joy, Brooke, and Helen for challenging my preconceptions about human cognition. I would also like to acknowledge all of the people who engaged in the conversations specifically recounted in this book, including: Joe Huseby, Paul Lenze, Jeff Rosky, and Philip Wiecko. Many thanks to Tom Carson-Knowles and Kaelyn Barron for their valuable contributions to this book. If I left anyone out it was either accidental or intentional because I don't like you.

ABOUT THE AUTHOR

Glen Smith is a professor of American Politics at the University of North Georgia, where he studies the causes and consequences of political hostility. His research has been published in academic journals such as *Public Opinion Quarterly, Political Research Quarterly, and American Politics Research*. In addition, he has contributed numerous posts to Newsweek, Yahoo, and PsyPost. His previous book is titled *Disagreeing Agreeably: Issue Debates with a Primer on Political Disagreement*.

ENDNOTES

1   Merriam-Webster
2   Smith 2020; Huber & Malhotra 2017
3   Pew Research, 2019
4   Wyatt et al. 2000; Eveland & Hively 2009
5   Brownstein 2008; Mann and Ornstein 2016; Drutman 2020
6   American Psychiatric Association, 2013
7   Iyengar et al., 2019
8   Iyengar et al., 2019
9   Pew Research Center, 2019
10 Drutman, 2020
11 Pew Research Center, 2020
12 Dimock & Wike, 2020
13 Pew Research Center, 2019
14 Kalmoe & Mason, 2019
15 Huber & Malhotra, 2017
16 Smith, 2020
17 Pesce, 2016; McCarthy, 2016; Holmes, 2017
18 Chen & Rohla, 2018
19 Huber & Malhotra, 2017
20 Nicholson et al., 2016
21 Drutman, 2017
22 Peterson & Iyengar, 2021
23 Bartels, 2002; Evans & Pickup, 2010; Schaffner & Roche, 2016
24 Gerber & Huber, 2010
25 Enns et al., 2012
26 McConnell et al., 2017
27 Gift & Gift, 2015
28 Iyengar & Westwood, 2015; Munro et al., 2010
29 Claassen & Ensley, 2016

30 Kalmoe & Mason, 2019; Diamond et al. 2020
31 Cassese, 2021; Martherus, et al. 2021
32 Tyson, 2020
33 Gollwitzer et al., 2020
34 V for Vendetta, 2005
35 Public Agenda, 2019
36 Anxiety & Depression Association of America, 2020
37 Anxiety & Depression Association of America, 2020
38 Green et al., 2002
39 Lench et al., 2019
40 Smith et al. 2019; APA 2020
41 Musse and Schneider 2022; Smith et al. 2019
42 Pew Research Center, 2019
43 Hart, 2018
44 Carlson, 2020
45 Abramowitz, 2012
46 Putnam, 2000
47 Levendusky, 2009
48 for a review, see Levendusky 2009
49 Abramowitz, 2012
50 Dottle, 2019; Wilkinson, 2019
51 Drutman, 2020
52 Dunn, 2020
53 Green et al., 2002
54 Gilens 1996
55 Sit 2018
56 Bacon, 2018
57 More In Common, 2019
58 Levendusky 2018
59 Carrega et al., 2020
60 Farley, 2021
61 Simon et al., 2021
62 Diamond et al., 2020
63 Abramowitz & Webster, 2018

64 Bankert, 2020
65 Layman et al., 2010
66 Drutman, 2017
67 Amira et al., 2021
68 Talk of the Nation, 2011
69 Cassese, 2021
70 Martherus et al., 2021
71 Lee & Quealy, 2019
72 Bacon, 2021
73 Shapiro, 2020
74 Dialectical Behavior Therapy, 2014
75 Adler, A. 2009
76 Kunda, 1990
77 Westen and colleagues, 2006
78 Taber and Lodge, 2006
79 Butler and Dynes, 2016
80 Robinson et al., 1995
81 Pronin et al. 2002; West et al., 2012
82 Pronin and Kugler, 2007
83 Church & Samuelson, 2017
84 Church & Samuelson, 2017
85 Leary et al., 2017; Porter & Schumann, 2018; Krumrei-Mancuso et al., 2020
86 Leary et al., 2017; Krumrei-Mancuso, 2017; Porter & Schumann, 2018
87 Church & Samuelson, 2017; Leary at el., 2017; Porter & Schumann, 2018
88 Kunda, 1990; Taber & Lodge, 2006
89 Leary et al. 2017
90 Church & Samuelson, 2017; Krumrei-Mancuso et al., 2020
91 Festinger, 1962
92 Hopkin et al. 2014
93 Church & Samuelson, 2017

94   Deffler et al., 2016; Leary et al., 2017; Porter & Schumann, 2018
95   Taber & Lodge, 2006; Taber et al., 2009
96   Strickler, 2018
97   Taber et al., 2009; Taber & Lodge, 2016
98   Reeder et al., 2005; Waytz et al., 2014
99   Church & Samuelson, 2017; Leary et al., 2017; Porter & Schumann, 2018

100   Ahler, 2014; Kennedy & Pronin, 2008; Sherman et al., 2003
101   Waytz et al., 2014
102   Mutz, 2002; Testa et al., 2014; Porter & Schumann, 2018
103   Church & Samuelson, 2017; Krumrei-Mancuso et al., 2020
104   Leary et al., 2017
105   Hook et al. 2017
106   Porter and Schumann 2018
107   Fernbach et al. 2013
108   David et al., 2018; Balkıs, M., & Duru, E. 2019
109   Turner 2016; Turner and Bennett, 2017
110   Ellis, 1991
111   Ellis & Doyle, 2019
112   Ibid
113   Ellis & Doyle, 2019, p. 85-86
114   Ellis & Doyle, 2019, p. 98
115   Ellis & Doyle, 2019, p. 97
116   Smith & Searles, 2014
117   Smith, 2016
118   Levendusky, 2014
119   Searles & Smith, 2016
120   Southern Poverty Law Center 2019
121   Yudkin et al., 2019
122   Yudkin et al., 2019

123   Cappella and Jamieson, 1997
124   Iyengar et al., 2004
125   Vallone et al. 1985; Feldman 2011
126   Hastorf and Cantril, 1954
127   Smith, 2010
128   Smith, 2017
129   Dimock & Wike, 2020
130   Abramowitz, 2012
131   Pew Research Center, 2014
132   Galston & Dionne, 2015
133   Halbridge & Malhotra, 2011
134   Boatright, 2013
135   Corbin, 2015
136   DeSilver, 2020
137   Galston & Dionne, 2015
138   Mann and Ornstein, 2012
139   Woodard, 2020
140   Pew Research Center, 2019
141   Scheufele, 2000; Wyatt et al., 2000
142   Price et al., 2002
143   Mutz, 2002
144   Huckfeldt & Sprague, 1987; Huckfeldt et al., 2004
145   Mutz, 2006
146   Brooks & Geer, 2007
147   Hwang et al., 2016
148   Mutz, 2015
149   Steele & Liu, 1983
150   Rios et al., 2014
151   Mill, J. S. 1869

REFERENCES

Abramowitz, A. I. (2012). The Polarized Public: Why American Government is so Dysfuctional. Pearson Higher Ed.

Abramowitz, A. I., & Webster, S. W. (2018). Negative Partisanship: Why Americans Dislike Parties But Behave Like Rabid Partisans. Political Psychology, 39, 119–135.

Adler, A. (2009). The Neurotic Constitution; Outlines of a Comparative Individualistic Psychology and Psychotherapy. New York: Routledge.

Ahler, D. J. (2014). Self-Fulfilling Misperceptions of Public Polarization. The Journal of Politics, 76(3), 607–620.

American Psychiatric Association. (2013). Diagnostic and Statistical Manual of Mental disorders (5th ed.). American Psychiatric Association.

American Psychological Association. (2020, October 7). "2020 Presidential election a source of significant stress for more Americans than 2016 presidential race." Retrieved from: https://www.apa.org/news/press/releases/2020/10/election-stress

Amira, K., Wright, J. C., & Goya-Tocchetto, D. (2021). In-Group Love Versus Out-Group Hate: Which Is More Important to Partisans and When? Political Behavior, 43(2), 473–494.

Anxiety & Depression Association of America. (2020).

Facts & Statistics. https://adaa.org/understanding-anxiety/facts-statistics#:~:text=Anxiety

Asch, S. E. (1956). Studies of independence and conformity: I. A minority of one against a unanimous majority. Psychological Monographs: General and Applied, 70(9), 1–70.

Bacon, P. Jr. (2018, June 26). Democrats Are Wrong About Republicans. Republicans Are Wrong About Democrats. FiveThirtyEight. https://fivethirtyeight.com/features/democrats-are-wrong-about-republicans-republicans-are-wrong-about-democrats/

Bacon, P., Jr. (2021, February 8). In America's "Uncivil War," Republicans Are The Aggressors. FiveThirtyEight. https://fivethirtyeight.com/features/in-americas-uncivil-war-republicans-are-the-aggressors/

Balkıs, M., & Duru, E. (2019). The protective role of rational beliefs on the relationship between irrational beliefs, emotional states of stress, depression and anxiety. Journal of Rational-Emotive & Cognitive-Behavior Therapy, 37(1), 96-112.

Bankert, A. (2020). Negative and Positive Partisanship in the 2016 U.S. Presidential Elections. Political Behavior, 1–19.

Bartels, L. M. (2002). Beyond the Running Tally: Partisan Bias in Political Perceptions. Political Behavior, 24(2), 117–150.

Boatright, R. G. (2013). Getting Primaried: The Changing Politics of Congressional Primary Challenges. Ann Arbor, MI: University of Michigan Press.

Brooks, D. J., & Geer, J. G. (2007). Beyond negativity: The effects of incivility on the electorate. American Journal of Political Science, 51(1):1-16.

Brownstein, Ronald. 2008. The second civil war: How extreme partisanship has paralyzed Washington and polarized America. New York: Penguin House.

Butler, D. M., & Dynes, A. M. (2016). How politicians discount the opinions of constituents with whom they disagree. American Journal of Political Science, 60(4), 975-989.

Cappella, Joseph N., and Kathleen Hall Jamieson. (1997). Spiral of cynicism: The press and the public good. New York: Oxford University Press.

Carlson, Tucker. (2020, July 7). Can the Left Really Lead a County it Hates? Fox News. https://www.foxnews.com/opinion/tucker-carlson-left-lead-country-hates

Carrega, C., Stracqualursi, V., & Campbell, J. (2020, October 8). 13 charged in plot to kidnap Michigan Gov. Gretchen Whitmer. CNN. https://www.cnn.com/2020/10/08/politics/fbi-plot-michigan-governor-gretchen-whitmer/index.html

Carsey, T. M., & Layman, G. C. (2004). Policy Balancing and Preferences for Party Control of Government. Political Research Quarterly, 57(4), 541–550.

Cassese, E. C. (2021). Partisan Dehumanization in American Politics. Political Behavior, 43(1), 29–50.

Chen, M. K., & Rohla, R. (2018). The effect of partisanship and political advertising on close family ties. Science,

360(6392), 1020–1024.

Church, I. M., & Samuelson, P. L. (2017). Intellectual Humility: An Introduction to the Philosophy and Science.

Claassen, R. L., & Ensley, M. J. (2016). Motivated Reasoning and Yard-Sign-Stealing Partisans: Mine is a Likable Rogue, Yours is a Degenerate Criminal. Political Behavior, 38(2), 317–335.

Clinton, J., Cohen, J., Lapinski, J., & Trussler, M. 2021. "Partisan pandemic: How partisanship and public health concerns affect individuals' social mobility during COVID-19." Science advances, 7(2), eabd7204.

Cookson, J. A., Engelberg, J. E., & Mullins, W. 2020. "Does partisanship shape investor beliefs? Evidence from the COVID-19 pandemic." The Review of Asset Pricing Studies, 10(4), 863-893.

Corbin, C. (2015, March 20). Constitution experts on Obama mandatory voting idea: Never gonna happen. Fox News. http://www.foxnews.com/politics/2015/03/20/mandatory-voting-experts.html

David, D., Cotet, C., Matu, S., Mogoase, C., & Stefan, S. 2018. "50 years of rational-emotive and cognitive-behavioral therapy: A systematic review and meta-analysis." Journal of Clinical Psychology, 74(3), 304–318.

Deffler, S. A., Leary, M. R., & Hoyle, R. H. 2016. "Knowing what you know: Intellectual humility and judgments of recognition memory." Personality and Individual

Differences, 96, 255–259.

Desilver, D. (2020, November 3). In past elections, U.S. trailed most developed countries in voter turnout. Pew Research Center. http://www.pewresearch. org/fact-tank/2017/05/15/u-s-voter-turnout-trails-most-developed-countries/

Dialectical Behavior Therapy. (2014). Psychology Today. https://www.psychologytoday.com/us/therapy-types/dialectical-behavior-therapy

Diamond, L., Drutman, L., Lindberg, T., Kalmoe, N. P., & Mason, L. (2020, October 1). Americans Increasingly Believe Violence is Justified if the Other Side Wins. Politico. https://www.politico.com/news/magazine/2020/10/01/political-violence-424157

Dimock, M., & Wike, R. (2020, November 13). America is exceptional in the nature of its political divide. Pew Research Center. https://www.pewresearch. org/fact-tank/2020/11/13/america-is-exceptional-in-the-nature-of-its-political-divide/?utm_content=buffer72091&utm_medium=social&utm_source=twitter.com&utm_campaign=buffer

Dottle, R. (2019, May 20). Where Democrats And Republicans Live In Your City. FiveThirtyEight. https://projects.fivethirtyeight.com/republicans-democrats-cities/

Drutman, L. (2017, September 5). We need political parties. But their rabid partisanship could destroy American democracy. Vox. https://www.vox.com/the-big-idea/2017/9/5/16227700/hyperpartisanship-identity-american-democracy-problems-solutions-doom-loop

Drutman, L. (2020, October 5). How Hatred Came To Dominate American Politics. FiveThirtyEight. https://fivethirtyeight.com/features/how-hatred-negative-partisanship-came-to-dominate-american-politics/

Drutman, L. (2020, September 22). The Republican and Democratic Parties Are Heading for Collapse. Foreign Policy. https://foreignpolicy.com/2020/09/22/two-party-collapse-republican-democrat-doom-loop/

Drutman, Lee. (2020). Breaking the two-party doom loop: The case for multiparty democracy in America. New York: Oxford University Press.

Dryden, W., DiGiuseppe, R., & Neenan, M. (2010). A primer on rational emotive behaviour therapy. Champaign, IL: Research Press.

Dunn, A. (2020, September 18). Few Trump or Biden supporters have close friends who back the opposing candidate. Pew Research Center. https://www.pewresearch.org/fact-tank/2020/09/18/few-trump-or-biden-supporters-have-close-friends-who-back-the-opposing-candidate/?utm_content=buffere822d&utm_medium=social&utm_source=twitter.com&utm_campaign=buffer

Egan, P. J. 2020. "Identity as Dependent Variable: How Americans Shift Their Identities to Align with Their Politics." American Journal of Political Science, 64(3), 699–716.

Ekstrom, P., Smith, B., Williams, A., & Kim, H. (2019, July 26). People who experience political disagreement with those who are close to them are less likely to follow the party line. LSE Phelan US Centre. *http:// bit.ly/2yaZM0C*

Ellis, A. 1991. "The revised ABC's of rational-emotive therapy (RET)." Journal of Rational-Emotive and Cognitive-Behavior Therapy, 9(3), 139-172.

Ellis, A., & Doyle, K. A. (2019). How To Control Your Anxiety Before It Controls You. Robinson.

Enns, P. K., Kellstedt, P. M., & McAvoy, G. E. 2012. "The Consequences of Partisanship in Economic Perceptions." Public Opinion Quarterly, 76(2), 287–310.

Evans, G., & Pickup, M. 2010. "Reversing the Causal Arrow: The Political Conditioning of Economic Perceptions in the 2000–2004 U.S. Presidential Election Cycle." The Journal of Politics, 72(4), 1236–1251.

Eveland, W. P., & Hively, M. H. 2009. "Political discussion frequency, network size, and "heterogeneity" of discussion as predictors of political knowledge and participation." Journal of Communication, 59(2):205-224.

Farley, G. (2021, February 16). Argument over political sign turns deadly in Skagit County, sheriff's office says. KING-TV. https://www.king5.com/article/ news/politics/woman-shot-killed-political-sign-washington-state/281-0e3fa007-183f-4600-acea-d0946f3c81f9

Feldman, Lauren. 2011. "Partisan differences in opinionated news perceptions: A test of the hostile media effect." Political Behavior 33(3): 407-432.

Fernbach, Philip M., Todd Rogers, Craig R. Fox, and Steven A. Sloman. 2013. "Political extremism is supported by an illusion of understanding." Psychological science, 24(6): 939-946.

Festinger, L. (1962). A theory of cognitive dissonance.

Galston, W. A., & Dionne, E. J., Jr. (2015, September 27). Should Voting Be Compulsory? Newsweek. http://www.newsweek.com/should-voting-be-compulsory-376905

Gerber, A. S., & Huber, G. A. 2010. "Partisanship, Political Control, and Economic Assessments." American Journal of Political Science, 54(1), 153–173.

Gift, K., & Gift, T. 2015. Does Politics Influence Hiring? Evidence from a Randomized Experiment. Political Behavior, 37(3), 653–675.

Gilens, M. 1996. "Race coding" and white opposition to welfare." American Political Science Review, 90(3), 593-604.

Gollwitzer, A., Martel, C., Brady, W. J., Knowles, E. D., & Bavel, J. V. 2020. "Partisan Differences in Physical Distancing Predict Infections and Mortality During the Coronavirus Pandemic." Available at: Social Science Research Network 3609392.

Goren, P. 2005. Party Identification and Core Political Values. American Journal of Political Science, 49(4), 881–896.

Green, D. P., Palmquist, B., & Schickler, E. (2002). Partisan

Hearts and Minds: Political Parties and the Social Identities of Voters. New Haven, CT: Yale University Press.

Gutmann, A., & Thompson, D. F. (1998). Democracy and disagreement. Harvard University Press, 1998.

Harbridge, L., & Malhotra, N. 2011. Electoral incentives and partisan conflict in congress: Evidence from survey experiments. American Journal of Political Science, 55(3), 494–510.

Hart, Kim. (2018, November 12). Exclusive Poll: Most Democrats see Republicans as Racist, Sexist. Axios. https://www.axios.com/poll-democrats-and-republicans-hate-each-other-racist-ignorant-evil-99ae7afc-5a51-42be-8ee2-3959e43ce320.html

Hastorf, Albert H., and Hadley Cantril. 1954. "They saw a game; a case study." The Journal of Abnormal and Social Psychology, 49(1):129.

Hensch, M. (2017, June 6). Eric Trump: Dems "not even people." The Hill. https://thehill.com/homenews/administration/336683-eric-trump-dems-not-even-people

Hirczy, W. (1994). The impact of mandatory voting laws on turnout: A quasi-experimental approach. Electoral Studies, 13(1), 64–76.

Hook, J. N., Farrell, J. E., Johnson, K. A., Tongeren, D. R. V., Davis, D. E., & Aten, J. D. (2017). Intellectual humility and religious tolerance. The Journal of Positive Psychology, 12(1), 29–35.

Hopkin, C. R., Hoyle, R. H., & Toner, K. (2014). Intellectual

Humility and Reactions to Opinions about Religious Beliefs. Journal of Psychology and Theology, 42(1), 50–61.

Hoyle, R. H., Davisson, E. K., Diebels, K. J., & Leary, M. R. (2016). Holding specific views with humility: Conceptualization and measurement of specific intellectual humility. Personality and Individual Differences, 97, 165–172.

Huber, G. A., & Malhotra, N. 2017. Political Homophily in Social Relationships: Evidence from Online Dating Behavior. The Journal of Politics, 79(1), 269–283.

Huckfeldt, R., & Sprague, J. 1987. Networks in Context: The Social Flow of Political Information. American Political Science Review, 81(4): 1197-1216.

Huckfeldt, R., Johnson, P. E., & Sprague, J. (2004). The Survival of Diverse Opinions within Communication Networks. Cambridge: Cambridge University Press.

Huckfeldt, R., Mendez, J. M., & Osborn, T. 2004. Disagreement, ambivalence and engagement: The political consequences of heterogeneous networks. Political Psychology, 25(1):65-95.

Hwang, H., Kim, Y., & Kim, Y. 2016. Influence of discussion incivility on deliberation: An examination of the mediating role of moral indignation. Communication Research, 45(2).

Iyengar, S., & Westwood, S. J. 2015. Fear and Loathing across Party Lines: New Evidence on Group Polarization. American Journal of Political Science, 59(3), 690–707.

Iyengar, S., Lelkes, Y., Levendusky, M., Malhotra, N., & Westwood, S. J. 2019. The Origins and Consequences of Affective Polarization in the United States. Annual Review of Political Science, 22(1), 129–146.

Iyengar, Shanto, Helmut Norpoth, and Kyu S. Hahn. 2004. "Consumer demand for election news: The horserace sells." The Journal of Politics, 66(1): 157-175.

Jones, P. E. (2020). Partisanship, Political Awareness, and Retrospective Evaluations, 1956–2016. Political Behavior, 42(4), 1295–1317.

Kalmoe, N. P., & Mason, L. (2019, January). Lethal Mass Partisanship: Prevalence, Correlates, & Electoral Contingencies. NCAPSA. American Politics Meeting. https://www.dannyhayes.org/uploads/6/9/8/5/69858539/kalmoe_mason_ncapsa_2019_-_lethal_partisanship_-_final_lmedit.pdf

Kennedy, K. A., & Pronin, E. (2008). When Disagreement Gets Ugly: Perceptions of Bias and the Escalation of Conflict. Personality and Social Psychology Bulletin, 34(6), 833–848.

Krumrei-Mancuso, E. J. (2017). Intellectual humility and prosocial values: Direct and mediated effects. The Journal of Positive Psychology, 12(1), 13–28.

Krumrei-Mancuso, E. J., Haggard, M. C., LaBouff, J. P., & Rowatt, W. C. (2020). Links between intellectual humility and acquiring knowledge. The Journal of Positive Psychology, 15(2), 155–170.

Kunda, Z. (1990). The case for motivated reasoning. Psychological Bulletin, 108(3), 480–498.

Layman, G. C., Carsey, T. M., Green, J. C., Herrera, R., & Cooperman, R. (2010). Activists and Conflict Extension in American Party Politics. American Political Science Review, 104(2), 324–346.

Leary, M. R., Diebels, K. J., Davisson, E. K., Jongman-Sereno, K. P., Isherwood, J. C., Raimi, K. T., … Hoyle, R. H. (2017). Cognitive and interpersonal features of intellectual humility. Personality and Social Psychology Bulletin, 43(6), 793–813.

Lee, J. C., & Quealy, K. (2019, May 24). The 598 People, Places and Things Donald Trump Has Insulted on Twitter: A Complete List. The New York Times. https://www.nytimes.com/interactive/2016/01/28/upshot/donald-trump-twitter-insults.html

Lench, H. C., Levine, L. J., Perez, K. A., Carpenter, Z. K., Carlson, S. J., & Tibbett, T. (2019). Changes in subjective well-being following the US Presidential election of 2016. Emotion, 19(1), 1.

Levendusky, M. (2009). The Partisan Sort: How Liberals Became Democrats and Conservatives Became Republicans. Chicago, IL: University of Chicago Press.

Levendusky, M. S. (2014). Ground Wars: Personalized Communication in Political Campaigns. Perspectives on Politics, 12(3), 746–747.

Levendusky, M. S. (2018). Americans, Not Partisans: Can Priming American National Identity Reduce Affective Polarization? The Journal of Politics, 80(1), 59–70.

Lyle, L. (2015, October). Political Anger is a Reflex.

The Positive Psychology People. https://www.thepositivepsychologypeople.com/political-anger-is-a-reflex/

Mann, T. E., & Ornstein, N. J. (2012, May 17). Want to end partisan politics? Here's what won't work — and what will. The Washington Post. (https://www.washingtonpost.com/opinions/want-to-end-partisan-politics-heres-what-wont-work--and-what-will/2012/05/17/gIQA5jqcWU_story.html

Mann, Thomas E., and Norman J. Ornstein. 2016. It's even worse than it looks: How the American constitutional system collided with the new politics of extremism. New York: Basic Books.

Martherus, J. L., Martinez, A. G., Piff, P. K., & Theodoridis, A. G. (2021). Party Animals? Extreme Partisan Polarization and Dehumanization. Political Behavior, 43(2): 517–540.

McClurg, S. D. (2006). The Electoral Relevance of Political Talk: Examining Disagreement and Expertise Effects in Social Networks on Political Participation. American Journal of Political Science, 50(3):737-54.

McConnell, C., Margalit, Y., Malhotra, N., & Levendusky, M. (2017, May 19). Research: Political Polarization Is Changing How Americans Work and Shop. Harvard Business Review. https://hbr.org/2017/05/research-political-polarization-is-changing-how-americans-work-and-shop

McLeod, J. M., Scheufele, D. A., & Moy, P. (1999). Community, communication, and participation: The role of mass media and interpersonal discussion in local political participation. Political Communication, 16(2): 315-336.

Merriam-Webster. (n.d.). Partisan. In Merriam-Webster. com dictionary. Retrieved May 24, 2021, from https://www.merriam-webster.com/dictionary/partisan

Mill, J. S. (1869). On liberty. Longmans, Green, Reader, and Dyer.

Miller, P. R., & Conover, P. J. (2015). Red and blue states of mind: Partisan hostility and voting in the United States. Political Research Quarterly, 68(2):225-239.

More In Common. (2019). The Perception Gap. https://perceptiongap.us/

Munro, G. D., Lasane, T. P., & Leary, S. P. (2010). Political Partisan Prejudice: Selective Distortion and Weighting of Evaluative Categories in College Admissions Applications. Journal of Applied Social Psychology, 40(9), 2434–2462.

Musse, Isabel and Schneider, Rodrigo. (2022). "The Effect of Presidential Election Outcomes on Alcohol Drinking." Social Science Research Network. Available at Error! Hyperlink reference not valid. http://dx.doi.org/10.2139/ssrn.3662663

Mutz, D. C. (2002). The consequences of cross-cutting networks for political participation. American Journal of Political Science, 46, 838-855.

Mutz, D. C. (2015). In-Your-Face Politics: The Consequences of Uncivil Media. Princeton, NJ: Princeton University Press.

Mutz, Diana C. (2006). Hearing the other side: Deliberative versus participatory democracy. New York: Cambridge University Press.

Mutz, Diana C., & Mondak, J. J. (2006). The workplace as a context for cross-cutting political discourse. Journal of Politics, 68(1):140-155.

Nicholson, S. P., Coe, C. M., Emory, J., & Song, A. V. (2016). The Politics of Beauty: The Effects of Partisan Bias on Physical Attractiveness. Political Behavior, 38(4), 883–898.

Orwell, G. (1942, August). Looking Back on the Spanish War. The Orwell Foundation. *https://www. orwellfoundation.com/the-orwell-foundation/orwell/ essays-and-other-works/looking-back-on-the-spanish-war/*

Peterson, E., & Iyengar, S. (2021). Partisan Gaps in Political Information and Information☒Seeking Behavior: Motivated Reasoning or Cheerleading? American Journal of Political Science, 65(1), 133–147.

Pew Research Center. (2014, October 31). The Party of Nonvoters. http://www.people-press. org/2014/10/31/the-party-of-nonvoters-2/

Pew Research Center. (2019). Partisan Antipathy: More Intense, More Personal. https://www.pewresearch. org/politics/2019/10/10/partisan-antipathy-more-intense-more-personal/

Pew Research Center. (2019, June 19). Public Highly Critical of State of Political Discourse in the U.S. *https://www.pewresearch.org/politics/2019/06/19/ public-highly-critical-of-state-of-political-discourse-in-*

the-u-s/

Pew Research Center. (2020). Amid Campaign Turmoil, Biden Holds Wide Leads on Coronavirus, Unifying the Country (p. 3). https://www.pewresearch.org/politics/2020/10/09/amid-campaign-turmoil-biden-holds-wide-leads-on-coronavirus-unifying-the-country/

Porter, T., & Schumann, K. (2018). Intellectual humility and openness to the opposing view. Self and Identity, 17(2), 139–162.

Price, V., Cappella, J. N., & Nir, L. (2002). Does disagreement contribute to more deliberative opinion? Political Communication, 19(1):95-112.

Pronin, E., & Kugler, M. B. (2007). Valuing thoughts, ignoring behavior: The introspection illusion as a source of the bias blind spot. Journal of Experimental Social Psychology, 43(4), 565-578.

Pronin, E., Lin, D. Y., & Ross, L. (2002). The bias blind spot: Perceptions of bias in self versus others. Personality and Social Psychology Bulletin, 28(3), 369-381.

Public Agenda. (2019). America's Hidden Common Ground on Divisiveness in American Public Life. https://www.publicagenda.org/reports/divisiveness-and-collaboration-in-american-public-life-a-hidden-common-ground-report/

Putnam, R. D. (2000). Bowling Alone: The Collapse and Revival of American Community.

Reeder, G. D., Pryor, J. B., Wohl, M. J. A., & Griswell, M. L. (2005). On Attributing Negative Motives to Others

Who Disagree With Our Opinions. Personality and Social Psychology Bulletin, 31(11):1498-1510.

Rios, K., DeMarree, K. G., & Statzer, J. (2014). Attitude certainty and conflict style: Divergent effects of correctness and clarity. Personality and Social Psychology Bulletin, 40(7):819-830.

Robinson, R. J., Keltner, D., Ward, A., & Ross, L. (1995). Actual versus assumed differences in construal:"Naive realism"in intergroup perception and conflict. Journal of personality and social psychology, 68(3), 404.

Schaffner, B. F., & Roche, C. (2016). Misinformation and Motivated Reasoning Responses to Economic News in a Politicized Environment. Public Opinion Quarterly, 81(1), 86–110.

Scheufele, D. A. (2000). Talk or conversation? Dimensions of interpersonal discussion and their implications for participatory democracy. Journalism & Mass Communication Quarterly, 77(4): 727-743.

Searles, K., & Smith, G. (2016). Who's the Boss? Setting the Agenda in a Fragmented Media Environment. International Journal of Communication, 10, 22.

Shapiro, J. (2020, May 1). Finding Goldilocks: A Solution for Black-and-White Thinking. Psychology Today. https://www.psychologytoday.com/us/blog/thinking-in-black-white-and-gray/202005/finding-goldilocks-solution-black-and-white-thinking

Simon, D., Kravarik, J., & Kallingal, M. (2021, January 3). Here's why rioters say they're gathering in Portland. CNN. https://www.cnn.com/2021/01/22/us/portland-riot-protesters-charged/index.html

Sit, R. (2018, January 12). Trump thinks only black people are on welfare, but really, white Americans receive most benefits. Newsweek. Retrieved from: https://www.newsweek.com/donald-trump-welfare-black-white-780252

Smith, G., & Searles, K. (2014). Who Let the (Attack) Dogs Out? New Evidence for Partisan Media Effects. Public Opinion Quarterly, 78(1), 71–99.

Smith, Glen. 2017. "Sympathy for the Devil: How Broadcast News Reduces Negativity Toward Political Leaders." American Politics Research, 45(1): 63-84.

Smith, Kevin B., Matthew V. Hibbing, and John R. Hibbing. (2019). "Friends, relatives, sanity, and health: The costs of politics." PloS one, 14(9).

Smith, T. (2020, October 27). "Dude, I'm Done": When Politics Tears Families And Friendships Apart. National Public Radio. https://www.npr.org/2020/10/27/928209548/dude-i-m-done-when-politics-tears-families-and-friendships-apart

Southern Poverty Law Center. (2019). Hate Map. https://www.splcenter.org/hate-map

Steele, C. M., & Liu, T. J. (1983). Dissonance processes as self-affirmation. Journal of Personality and Social Psychology, 45(1):5-19.

Taber, C. S., & Lodge, M. (2006). Motivated Skepticism in the Evaluation of Political Beliefs. American Journal of Political Science, 50(3), 755–769.

Taber, C. S., & Lodge, M. (2016). The Illusion of Choice in Democratic Politics: The Unconscious Impact of

Motivated Political Reasoning. Political Psychology, 37, 61–85.

Taber, C. S., Cann, D., & Kucsova, S. (2009). The Motivated Processing of Political Arguments. Political Behavior, 31(2), 137–155.

Talk of the Nation. (2011, March 29). "Less Than Human": The Psychology Of Cruelty. National Public Radio. https://www.npr.org/2011/03/29/134956180/criminals-see-their-victims-as-less-than-human

Testa, P. F., Hibbing, M. V., & Ritchie, M. (2014). Orientations toward Conflict and the Conditional Effects of Political Disagreement. The Journal of Politics, 76(3), 770–785.

Turner, M. J. (2016). Rational emotive behavior therapy (REBT), irrational and rational beliefs, and the mental health of athletes. Frontiers in psychology, 7, 1423.

Turner, M., & Bennett, R. (Eds.). (2017). Rational emotive behavior therapy in sport and exercise. New York: Routledge.

Tyson, A. (2020, July 22). Republicans remain far less likely than Democrats to view COVID-19 as a major threat to public health. Pew Research Center. https://www.pewresearch.org/fact-tank/2020/07/22/republicans-remain-far-less-likely-than-democrats-to-view-covid-19-as-a-major-threat-to-public-health/

V for Vendetta. (2005). Warner Brothers.

Vallone, Robert P., Lee Ross, and Mark R. Lepper. 1985. "The hostile media phenomenon: biased perception and perceptions of media bias in coverage of the Beirut massacre." Journal of personality and social psychology, 49(3): 577.

Washington, G. (1976, Sept. 19). Farewell Address. National Archives. https://founders.archives.gov/documents/Washington/05-20-02-0440-0002

Waytz, A., Young, L. L., & Ginges, J. (2014). Motive attribution asymmetry for love vs. hate drives intractable conflict. Proceedings of the National Academy of Sciences of the United States of America, 111(44), 15687–15692.

West, R. F., Meserve, R. J., & Stanovich, K. E. (2012). Cognitive sophistication does not attenuate the bias blind spot. Journal of personality and social psychology, 103(3), 506.

Westen, D., Blagov, P. S., Harenski, K., Kilts, C., & Hamann, S. (2006). Neural Bases of Motivated Reasoning: An fMRI Study of Emotional Constraints on Partisan Political Judgment in the 2004 U.S. Presidential Election. Journal of Cognitive Neuroscience, 18(11), 1947–1958.

Wilkinson, W. (2019). The Density Divide: Urbanization, Polarization, and Population Backlash. Niskanen Center.

Woodard, C. (2020, February 19). Half of Americans Don't Vote. What Are They Thinking? Politico. https://www.politico.com/news/magazine/2020/02/19/knight-nonvoter-study-decoding-2020-election-wild-card-115796

Wyatt, R. O., Katz, E., & Kim, J. (2000). Bridging the spheres:

Political and personal conversation in public and
private spaces. Journal of Communication, 50(1):71-
92.

Yudkin, D., Hawkins, S., & Dixon, T. (2019). The
Perception Gap. The Perception Gap; More In
Common. https://perceptiongap.us/

CONNECT WITH GLEN SMITH

Sign up for Glen's newsletter at
www.disagreeingagreeably.com/newsletter

To find out more information visit his website:
www.disagreeingagreeably.com

Social media:

@GlenSmi70330487

@glenrsmith

BOOK DISCOUNTS AND SPECIAL DEALS

Sign up for free to get discounts and special deals
on our bestselling books at
www.TCKpublishing.com/bookdeals